GRAY DIVORCE
Silver Linings

A Woman's Guide to Divorce After 50

Acknowledgment

This book has not come easy. It was made possible through my own divorce experience, as well as my experience working with the many brave women struggling through the trials and tribulations of their own mid- to late-life divorces. Without your experience, and your voice, this book would not have been possible. Each and every one of you has taught me something about courage, tenacity and healing as you build the promising next chapters of your lives.

I also owe a debt of gratitude to my colleagues at the Stearns Financial Group for their unwavering support of me during the book writing process. Top among the list is Dennis Stearns, my partner and colleague, who conceived of the book and believed in its value. Next is the dedicated team that actually made the book possible – Christina, Michele, Sarah, Glenn, Keith, Tara and Bill. I'm deeply grateful to you.

Finally, I'd like to thank my editor, Martin Wilcox, who helped me find my voice.

To Jim and Maggie –

Through life's ups and downs, all things are possible.

Contents

CHAPTER ONE

Gray Divorce
Redefining the Golden Years

I had my whole life planned out at the age of fourteen, or so I thought.

I knew, for example, that I would go to college, have a career, get married, and raise a family. Like my mother, and her mother before her, I knew I would be successful in the things that really mattered to me, like my marriage and my family, as I prized these above all else.

Although I knew on some level that divorce was a risk, I never really believed it was a risk for *me*. In my mind, divorce happened only to *those* women – you know, the ones who somehow couldn't hold it all together. Maybe they had let themselves go. Or maybe they had addiction problems. Or maybe they had simply married the wrong person. Whatever the case, I knew I wasn't one of *those* women. I had taken every precaution and had done everything right. I had married a man who came from a loving family, someone who had good values. He was smart and generous. He was ambitious and so was I. We had similar goals and values. We both wanted children and we both wanted to succeed. Over the course of the next 23 years, we built a home, a family, and a life.

Then, in the summer of 2008, without warning, my husband coolly informed me that he was no longer "happy."

Long pause.

Those words, so simply spoken, hung in the air for what seemed an eternity. I simply could not comprehend them. In fact, I could hardly breathe. At that moment, my life changed forever.

Somehow, I had just become one of *those* women. Lying face down on the bathroom floor, I contemplated the following: *Would I be alone for the rest of my life? How would I protect my children? How would I take care of myself — of us?*

My sense of loss was unending. I had lost my husband. I had lost my innocent view of the world. I had lost the integrity of the family we once shared. From that day forward, holidays would never be the same. Our children would be split in their allegiances and would struggle with the very meaning of the words *family* and *home*.

In addition to the overwhelming changes that accompanied my new status, I harbored an excruciating sense of shame. I would be the first divorced woman in my immigrant family. I could still hear my 4'11" mother, towering over me, pointing her finger in my face as she said those unbearable words, "I told you so."

"Americans get divorced," she would say. This was a running debate during my formative years. I would mumble something about how Americans may divorce, but the rest of the world just suffers in silence. Now, for the first time, I wondered which was worse. The destruction of the family that had taken almost 25 years to build was unfathomable to me. I wondered if my husband realized what he was giving up, or whether he understood that "new" families simply cannot be manufactured.

Shocked as I was by the circumstances surrounding the end of my marriage, I should likely have seen it coming long before it did. It was my intense desire to keep my family together that blinded me to the realities of the marriage and the different values we had each embraced. In short, I had valued our family and all that it entailed: evening meals together, family game nights and trips to the zoo. Unfortunately, these were not to be. Rather, my husband had relentlessly pursued his career, taken positions in other cities, and vacationed two to three weeks a year with friends. Perhaps he, too, recognized that we had grown apart. Perhaps he, too, was lonely. Whatever the case, he continually put "us" at the bottom of his priority list.

I objected, of course. And objected some more. But as the years went on, my objections increasingly fell on deaf ears, until finally, they stopped all together. More and more, I expected nothing and said nothing. Yet, with each turning of the eye, I betrayed a part of myself until, in my silence, I lost my voice entirely.

In the end, I felt I had sacrificed my youth and my soul for a failed dream. I didn't have a vision for any future that excluded the "perfect" family we had created. All I had was a painful past. In addition, I had given up my career to raise our children. How would I move forward? How would I take care of them, or myself?

Over the course of the next five years, I embarked on a journey that began with survival, but gradually, almost imperceptibly, shifted toward one of self-discovery. I began to understand that we could not only take care of ourselves, but that we could thrive. I was determined not to be defined by my divorce, particularly in the eyes of my children. They needed to understand that hardships are a part of every life, but it is our response to these hardships that defines our character. This would be an important lesson for them, and if I succeeded, it would free them to pursue their lives without worrying about me.

This is not to say that it was easy. It wasn't. Not only was I the single parent of two teenaged children, I increasingly found myself socially isolated. I escaped to Italy for several weeks to study art, bought and renovated a historic home, and embarked on a professional career. I put myself "out there," in each and every case accepting the risk of further failure, but always hopeful that I would find meaning again.

I was the only woman I knew in this impossible situation. Who, other than my husband, would choose to start over again at this age? The answer, it turned out, was a whopping 600,000 people in 2010 alone. Even worse, based on current trends, the number of divorces over the age of 50, termed *gray divorce*, was expected to exceed 800,000 *per year* by 2030. Shockingly, I learned that not only was gray divorce on the rise, it was growing at more than double the rate of overall divorce in the United States. And these divorces were being initiated by women 66% of the time.[1] Given the emotional abandonment I had endured throughout my marriage, I could relate to this statistic.

---

[1] S.G. Thomas, March 3, 2012, *Divorce Late in Life: The Gray Divorces. Wall Street Journal*, retrieved from www.wsj.com

I thought back to my grandmother's, and even my mother's generation: for them, divorce was simply not an option. Something had changed dramatically. A bit more research revealed that several things had changed, the most significant of which included the rising financial independence of women. Coupled with the broad social acceptance of divorce and the general unwillingness to accept a less-than-perfect life, it made sense that divorce was prevalent, but it still didn't explain the root cause of divorce *after* the age of 50.

Determined to more fully understand this concept, I kept digging. I learned that baby boomers were the first generation to divorce and remarry in large numbers as young adults. Because second marriages fail at two-and-a-half times the rate of first marriages, it made sense that divorce rates were soaring as baby boomers aged. Simply put, boomers' complex marital biographies made them far more likely to divorce as they approached middle age.[2]

Still, I felt that after a certain age, divorce would simply stop being an option, regardless of marital biography. Not so. The rise in gray divorce goes to an even more fundamental shift: a change in our belief about life expectancy. We Americans, by and large, are living longer and healthier lives. Average life expectancies in the United States have increased by a full 10 years since 1960 alone, and the trend upward is continuing. Advances in medical technology and our own self-

[2]Lin, Brown & Hammersmith, November 1, 2015, Marital Biography, Social Security, and Poverty. *National Center for Family & Marriage Research Working Paper Series. Bowling Green State University,* retrieved from https://www.bgsu.edu

care continue to increase not only our longevity, but our sense of well-being in later life.

To put the impact of this trend into tangible terms, think back for a moment to your grandparents. In that generation, retirement often signaled the beginning of the end. Perhaps there would be another 10 to 15 years of life, but at least half of them would be spent in poor health. One spouse typically cared for the other, often accelerating her or his own decline.

Today, however, age 65 is considered young. Most new retirees, regardless of gender, believe they will live another 25 or even 30 years. They believe they will not only live longer, but be healthy enough to travel, start new careers, pursue their childhood dreams, and even find new partners with whom to share the rest of their lives.

Armed with this new knowledge, I began to put my own marriage and divorce into a new context. I, too, would have the opportunity to build a new life. I still had decades to pursue my own dreams, and perhaps even find a new partner. Given the number of women going through gray divorce, I suddenly didn't feel so alone. In fact, I began to wonder what we women would collectively represent. As a group, women currently control 83% of consumer spending and 51% of the nation's wealth. By 2030, it is estimated that women will control as much as two-thirds of the nation's wealth, fueled in large part by their own earnings, generational transfers, and, yes, spousal transfers resulting from gray divorce.[3] I suddenly realized that never in history have women wielded such power. I was curious to see how this new breed of woman: mature, single, and well-

---

[3]Women of Wealth White Paper, Heather R. Ettinger and Eileen M. O'Connor.

heeled, would impact society. But, before getting carried away with this theme, I realized that I would first have to find my way through the painful divorce that faced me. The challenge was daunting. For the first time, my husband and best friend was not on my "team." I felt overwhelmed and overpowered by him, realizing that he held not only all of the earnings power, but also, a sole knowledge of our financial situation.

As I made my way through this process, I also began to understand how vulnerable women in this situation are, and how difficult it is to get *financial* advice specific to divorce. Fortunately, I had a financial background and was able to understand the implications of the various settlement options before me. In the years to come, however, I would meet many divorcing women who would not be so fortunate.

Sadly, women of gray divorce are at risk of irreparable financial harm, often accepting settlements that are unequal and unfair. In some cases, a dependent woman still trusts that her husband will do what is right for her and simply accepts what is being offered. In other cases, illiquid, difficult-to-value, or hard-to-find assets are simply left behind, with the woman either too tired or too overwhelmed to pursue them. Whatever the cause, I cannot stress enough the importance of negotiating a fair settlement.

Numerous studies indicate that following a divorce, men continue to build their net worth, often acquiring and even exceeding their married standards of living, while women do not.[4] The evidence is clear, as are the causes. Leaving the negotiating table with fewer assets than their husbands, with

---

[4]https://www.theguardian.com/lifeandstyle/2009/jan/25/divorce-women-research

little to no ability to generate a meaningful income, and often fearful of financial markets, women lag behind in increasing, or even maintaining, their assets in the face of inflation. The long-term impact on a woman's financial security is, of course, devastating. It was ultimately this realization that led my colleagues and I to develop a practice devoted exclusively to assisting women and their attorneys negotiate equitable distributions.

If you find yourself facing a late-life divorce – alone and afraid – worried about your financial well-being, lacking a clear sense of what your marital estate is worth, unsure about how to participate in the impending negotiations, and struggling to create a new life for yourself – this book will help. Based on the personal experiences of women just like you, this book provides a step-by-step guide on how to:

- Select the divorce process that best suits your needs (Chapter 2),
- Build a divorce team that works exclusively for you (Chapter 3),
- Determine the size of your marital estate (Chapter 4),
- Negotiate an appropriate settlement (Chapter 5),
- Plan your financial future (Chapter 6),
- Trust your gut instincts when investing (Chapter 7),
- Understand the fundamentals of investing (Chapter 8), and
- Move beyond your divorce (Chapter 9).

Finally, before embarking on your journey, a word of encouragement. You may not be able to see past your current situation, but believe me when I say your future is bright. Women of gray divorce are forging ahead, embracing life, career, and relationships with the wisdom borne of their life experiences, both good and bad. Armed with passion and determination, these independent women are redefining the stereotypes of prior generations while, often unknowingly, completely redefining themselves.

CHAPTER TWO

Selecting Your Divorce Process

If you're reading this book, you're likely in the midst of a mid- to late-life divorce. Understanding how you fit into the gray divorce phenomenon may help put things into a broader perspective, but it will not likely ease your emotional suffering nor calm the chaos that has become your life. Getting over your divorce will require time, distance, and perspective. Unfortunately, the divorce process will not afford you any of these luxuries: rather, you will be forced to make legal and financial decisions that will impact the rest of your life – *now*. While it may be tempting to simply accept whatever is being offered rather than face the uncertainty and anxiety of further negotiations, agreeing to a "do-it-yourself" settlement without fully understanding either the marital estate or the long-term implications is a decision most women quickly regret.

As such, it is critical to surround yourself with a team of professionals who can help you navigate the divorce process effectively. Not only do these professionals bring experience to the table, but they also bring a rational sensibility that is virtually impossible to achieve alone, given the emotional trauma of the divorce.

This chapter will focus on the legal professionals available to help you, as your first decision point will be the selection of a legal process. This decision, especially nuanced for gray divorcers, will impact not only you and your husband, but also your adult children, as well as the entire extended family. It is vital, therefore, to be aware of the different processes available and make a thoughtful decision before proceeding.

There are basically three different processes through which to divorce, each offering a distinct experience: litigation, characterized as an adversarial process; mediation, and collaborative divorce approaches, both characterized as non-adversarial. It's important for you to understand each process before determining which best suits your needs.

Take the time to research the different processes outlined below and interview at least one attorney who specializes in each type. Be wary of any attorney who claims to work in all three processes, because each type of divorce requires a different set of skills to ensure success.

Litigation

The vast majority of divorces are litigated, making this traditional process by far the most prevalent. Note that litigation is an adversarial process that will theoretically result in going to court. In fact, however, the overwhelming majority of divorce litigations settle out of court, precisely to avoid this outcome, because going to court will ultimately result in a judge deciding the resolution of the case rather than the couple themselves.

That said, litigation is not an easy process, especially for long-time marrieds. Because each party to the divorce is interested only in his or her own best outcome, trust and civility can quickly be drained out of the already teetering relationship. This is exacerbated by the fact that most of the communication occurs between two opposing attorneys on behalf of their clients.

Often, litigation can also be the most expensive option. Depending on how cooperative (or uncooperative) your spouse is, a litigated divorce can be drawn out for months and even years. The use of attorneys, outside experts, and witnesses can quickly add up to a small fortune.

On the emotional side, the process of litigation – which often includes subpoenas, depositions, and court appearances – is extremely difficult. This barrage of negativity can last for months, if not years. Often, any semblance of goodwill left between you and your spouse will quickly disappear, being replaced instead by suspicion and anger. For adults who have been married a lifetime and who share children, litigation and its negative emotional consequences can often damage the entire family, making it difficult to maintain civility going forward.

In addition to the damage caused to the relationship between you and your spouse and the extended family, understand that a difficult litigation can emotionally damage you as well. In my experience, women who have been through such an ordeal are often truly traumatized, unable to view even the best years of the marriage with fondness.

As you contemplate your options, consider the emotional toll and whether it's worth it to you. If a non-adversarial legal process can yield a fair settlement for you, don't rule it out. Don't simply choose litigation because you're trying to get even with your spouse. Rather, consider the consequences to yourself.

With that said, for many women, litigation is the only way to ensure an adequate outcome. This is true especially if you don't trust your spouse, or feel he might hide assets or withhold important information that will prevent you from getting a fair settlement. Often, the more complex the marital estate, the more likely litigation will be the only option. Examples include marital estates with significant assets, hard-to-value business interests, and complex and often disputed assets, such as those received as either a gift or inheritance.

In my experience, the majority of high-net-worth divorces are resolved through litigation, simply because there is so much money at stake. Some settle out of court, some don't.

Remember, however, that if you end up in court, it will be a judge, not you and your spouse, that will determine the ultimate outcome of your settlement.

Finally, a word of caution. If you find yourself in an adversarial divorce process, don't wait to begin interviewing and retaining top family law litigators. We've seen far too many cases where the wife is unable to obtain legal representation because the husband has already met with multiple local attorneys. Once this happens, you will be "conflicted" out of working with any of these attorneys, even if your husband ends up using someone else!

If you don't fit the profile of most litigated cases, you and your spouse may consider one of the following non-adversarial options, both of which require open communication and the transparent sharing of information between the divorcing couple. The goal of both processes is to leave one another as whole as possible, with minimal damage to what is left of the relationship and the marital estate.

Mediation

Divorce mediation involves negotiations between only the divorcing couple and a neutral mediator, who may or may not be an attorney. The role of the mediator is to help the divorcing couple reach a mutually acceptable arrangement by providing potential solutions, setting ground rules, and facilitating communication. However, because the mediator is a neutral party, he or she cannot provide legal advice to either party. For relatively simple cases, mediation may be a good method. However, the risk of mediation is that one or both parties may not fully understand their legal rights upon the signing of an agreement. For this reason, it is imperative that you have the terms of any proposal or agreement reviewed by an independent family-law attorney who works exclusively for you. This will ensure that you are receiving at least the minimum amount that the laws of your state require. Also, have a financial professional review the proposed asset division. It is often the division of assets that can turn a seemingly fair settlement into one that actually favors the husband.

Remember, this process requires an open and honest disclosure of all marital assets, which can often times create an imbalance of power since it is most likely the husband who controls the "purse strings" and has an intimate knowledge of the finances.

Collaborative Divorce

The need for independent legal advice while in mediation is precisely why collaborative divorce is gaining momentum. It, too, is a non-adversarial process, though in this case each party to the divorce has his or her own legal representation. Similar to mediation, the divorcing couple will go through a series of meetings together in order to create an agreement that is amenable to each. In collaborative divorce, however, each party to the divorce is accompanied and represented by a collaborative divorce attorney who will help the client voice his or her needs while also providing legal counsel. The process culminates in a legal separation agreement that includes property division, spousal support, and child-custody provisions, if applicable. Again, in more complex cases, a financial professional may be employed to serve as a neutral. The financial neutral is charged with the task of creating a win-win solution. For very difficult situations, one or both parties may also have a divorce "coach," a mental-health professional who is there to support his or her client during the process.

Both mediation and collaborative divorce can be resolved more quickly, and often more cheaply, than litigation. As you might expect, however, the success of these non-adversarial processes is highly dependent on the skill and experience of the professionals involved. Let's face it – it's not easy to resolve conflict between a couple who is divorcing. Tremendous skill and experience is required to assist them in reaching a just settlement.

For this reason, it is imperative to use board-certified mediators and collaborative attorneys who practice non-adversarial divorce processes exclusively. It is rare to find a litigator who can assume the role of a mediator or collaborative attorney effectively, although many try. Such attorneys can easily become combative during difficult negotiations, completely undermining the success of the process.

If a resolution cannot be reached, the parties can elect to end the process and pursue alternative divorce methods such as litigation. Note, however, that the attorneys working on the collaborative case are prohibited from representing their clients in a litigated divorce proceeding. This is to ensure that all parties are putting forth their best-faith effort to reach a successful outcome. If the process does not work, each party to the divorce will need to seek alternate representation, essentially starting the divorce process all over again.

With that said, if you and your spouse can both be open and transparent throughout the process, and if you are both willing to accept a fair outcome with less cost and less hostility, then collaborative divorce may be an excellent option for you. In our practice, we have seen both parties to a collaborative divorce walk away satisfied, feeling they each received a fair settlement and did the right thing for one another. This is no small achievement and goes a long way toward maintaining an amicable relationship in the years to come.

Regardless of the option you select, always ensure that your attorney is experienced, has a good track record, and is highly-credentialed. Most importantly, be sure you have a good rapport with your attorney. Divorce is difficult enough without having to endure it with a professional you don't like.

Jane

I had never heard of collaborative divorce when I began my research and was happy to find a quick and quiet way to settle the finances without the threat of litigation. I preferred this method to mediation, since it ensured I would have legal representation without going to court. I ultimately made an appointment with a well-respected collaborative attorney who confirmed my best hopes. She was warm and approachable, non-combative, and reassuring. She told me that collaborative divorce was an excellent way to create win-win scenarios and that it often resulted in sustainable settlements. However, she also mentioned that the process required full and open disclosure by both parties.

When I told her that Bill had already made a generous offer that included enough alimony to cover my expenses while also allowing me to keep the family home, she was encouraged. However, Bill's refusal to share information about his company gave her significant pause. The attorney told me that I was entitled to half the value of the company that Bill had built throughout our marriage. She said that if Bill would cooperate on this, she would be happy to represent me. If, however, he was unwilling to provide information surrounding the business, then it would likely be best to go the traditional route of litigation, particularly since the business represented the bulk of our marital estate.

This was not what I wanted to hear. I explained again that Bill had already made a very generous settlement offer and that I was happy to simply accept it. I explained that if I pushed too hard, he might cut me off financially and, even worse, retract his offer. I was also concerned about our girls and worried that I would make things harder for them by litigating. Bill would be furious and he would be sure to blame me for everything, especially since I was the one who wanted out of the marriage.

Although the attorney understood my reasoning and agreed that this was ultimately my decision, she asked if I would consider seeing a financial professional who specializes in divorce. "Just make certain that the settlement you are being offered will sustain you for the rest of your life. At this age," she said, "you can't afford to make a mistake." She explained that, statistically speaking, men continue to improve their economic standing subsequent to a divorce while women typically decline economically, in spite of receiving seemingly generous settlements. She *explained that what may look good on the surface may have poor long-term consequences. I reluctantly agreed to see a financial professional who specialized in divorce before making any decisions about either the settlement or the legal process I would pursue. In truth, however, I was afraid of taking such a bold step. I worried that Bill would be livid if he found out.*

CHAPTER THREE

Build Your Team

Now that you've considered your legal options, and potentially selected an attorney to represent you, let's focus on building the rest of your team. As a divorcing woman over the age of 50, you have a specific fact pattern that impacts your negotiating ability. For example, you likely have adult children and deep ties to the extended family, all of which puts pressure on you to settle quickly and fairly. Let's not forget, of course, the deep, complex ties you have to your husband. Patterns of behavior learned throughout a long-term marriage are difficult to break and can potentially undermine your ability to stand up for yourself, or even view your situation objectively.

Adding insult to injury, you also have less time to rectify a financial mistake during your divorce. If you have side-tracked your career to raise a family, you may also have limited earnings power. With the stakes so high, it is critical to seek out professionals who understand the nuances of gray divorce and can effectively advise you on the unique financial issues you face.

While every situation is different, your divorce team will likely be made up of at least two professionals in addition to your family-law attorney. Let's review these professionals.

Financial Professional

Though it might not be your first instinct to hire a financial professional as a part of your divorce team, he or she can be an invaluable addition. Let's face it, when going through a gray divorce, most issues surrounding child custody are no longer relevant. The real issue relating to a gray divorce is the financial settlement.

Given that most women in gray divorce are beyond their prime earning years, a settlement that is too low or unfair will ultimately prove disastrous financially, even if it seems generous today. It is extremely difficult to evaluate the adequacy of a settlement without fully understanding and quantifying your long-term financial needs, including the impact of taxes, inflation, and healthcare costs. In addition, you will need a thorough understanding of the marital estate in order to assess the tax implications of any proposed asset division. Even if you're receiving exactly half of an asset, you may be receiving less than half depending on the tax implications.

We sometimes see women who want to use their family investment manager or accountant to help them navigate their divorce. Note that it will be impossible for this individual to represent your best interests when he or she was likely hired by your husband and is still working for him as well as you. These family advisors may want to keep both you and your husband as clients following the divorce and will likely attempt to keep both of you happy. For the process of advising you through your divorce, we recommend you hire an independent financial professional who works exclusively for you, and preferably with your attorney. If you are using a non-adversarial process, it's equally important to use a neutral financial advisor, with no current or former relationship to either party.

We further advise that your financial professional and attorney contract with one another on your behalf. Not only will this result in a coordinated approach to your case, but it will also insure that, if you go to litigation, your husband's attorney will not be able to call your financial professional to the witness stand. If your attorney is unwilling to work with a financial professional, you should question why. After all, the financial aspect is at the core of your gray divorce, and ultimately your area of greatest need. If you're unable or unwilling to convince your attorney to coordinate efforts with your financial professional, you have two options: you can hire a different attorney, or you can independently seek out the help of a financial advisor and share the results with your attorney prior to negotiations. At a minimum, have your financial professional review the proposed settlement prior to signing any agreement.

When looking for financial assistance, remember that not every financial professional will do. In fact, you will need a professional who *specializes* in divorce. Divorce planning is a highly-nuanced aspect of financial planning and one that requires not only a credentialed professional, but one with substantial divorce experience. Be certain to ask your potential advisor the following questions: How many divorce cases have you had? Do you typically work with attorneys? What size settlements have you dealt with? Will you be able to testify in court, if necessary? Have you dealt with business holdings? If so, what size?

In addition to experience, we recommend your advisor have one of the following designations:

CFP® (Certified Financial Planner™). This is the highest designation in financial planning and involves a rigorous course of study, passage of the comprehensive CFP® Certification Examination, and three years of work experience.

CPA (Certified Public Accountant). This is the highest designation in the field of accounting and includes a rigorous course of study, passage of the Uniform Certified Public Accounting Examination, and, depending on the state of licensure, two years of work experience in either audit or tax.

CDFA (Certified Divorce Financial Analyst). This designation is newer and requires three years of experience in the financial services field, in addition to the passage of a comprehensive exam.

Again, keep in mind that the designation alone won't qualify your advisor. You will need someone with a proven track record of working with complex divorce cases.

Mental Health Professional

Let's face it – ending a long-term marriage will be among the most difficult experiences of your life. Feelings of anger, regret, inadequacy, abandonment, and betrayal are common and compounded by the impact of your divorce on your children, grandchildren, and extended family. I talked so much about my divorce to my friends and family that I was delighted to pay someone to listen when others simply no longer could. Regardless of how you ended up here, it's extremely helpful to discuss your situation with a trained professional. A good, empathetic therapist can be a lifeline leading up to, going through, and healing from the divorce.

Jane

Even though Jane was raised in a very traditional home and was totally committed to her husband, Bill, she couldn't escape the feelings of loneliness that increasingly plagued her marriage. In fact, she had felt emotionally isolated for most of her 30-year marriage. These feelings had become increasingly prevalent when the younger of their two daughters went away to college.

The problem, she realized, was that Bill was simply not present emotionally. In addition, the years of child-rearing and hard work had masked the fact that they could no longer communicate effectively or honestly. Although Jane openly acknowledged that Bill's drive and ambition were things that initially attracted her to him, she also now realized that no amount of success, money, or status could substitute for the intimate emotional connection she craved.

In spite of her best efforts, Jane simply could not reconcile herself to the status quo. Increasingly, she became depressed, and often had trouble even getting out of bed in the morning. Bill noticed Jane's "lazy" behavior and suggested she "get a life." He resented Jane's constant "nagging." Having worked hard over the past 30 years, Bill felt he had more than provided a comfortable lifestyle for his family. He simply could not understand what more Jane could want.

Jane tried to explain her feelings to Bill, and even suggested marriage counseling. He didn't have time for such "nonsense" and suggested Jane start playing tennis with the women at the club. Surely, this would help Jane move on from the loss of the children until she adjusted to her new life.

Though Jane had occasionally contemplated a divorce, she had never dreamed of actually going through with it. The thought of being without a husband terrified her; she didn't know if she could live with the stigma of being a divorcee; **and** *Bill had been the primary breadwinner for almost the entire length of their marriage. How could she possibly support herself without him?*

As the months slipped by, Jane slowly came to feel that through the course of their relationship, Bill – now president and majority shareholder of a growing software company – had cared more about his career than her.

Despondent and depressed, Jane decided to seek therapy. She knew she needed to change something in order to survive but could see no path forward. After months of therapy and soul-searching, Jane finally was able to acknowledge that she wanted more from life than the distant relationship she had with Bill. With her therapist's support, Jane ultimately approached Bill about a divorce. He was incensed. Not only did he consider her completely ungrateful for all that he had done, but now she would be after half of his net worth! Financially, their largest asset was Bill's partnership interest in the software company. Jane did not know the exact value of the company, but felt it was worth at least several million dollars. She knew the company had been very successful over the previous five years and had recently surged in value with the development of a new technology.

Despite the fact that the business was clearly a marital asset, Bill felt strongly that Jane was not entitled to any of his company. He had been the one working for the past 25 years, not her! He refused to share any information about the company with Jane and repeatedly told her that she would have to take him to court to get anything at all. He offered her half of the marital estate, excluding the value of the partnership interest, and he included what he considered a generous alimony for a period of 10 years. He also was willing to give her the home.

Jane couldn't imagine going to court. She had no money with which to hire an attorney. She feared if she pressed too hard, Bill would not only cut her off financially, but change his mind about the settlement he had already offered.

Jane discussed Bill's offer with her therapist, explaining her fear that Bill would cut her off financially if she pursued any interest in the business. Feeling uneasy, Jane explained that a collaborative attorney had advised her to seek financial advice before agreeing to any settlement.

With her therapist's help and support, Jane ultimately made an appointment with a reputable financial advisor who specialized in divorce. Jane continued to see her therapist, checking in with updates and bouncing her thoughts off someone who now knew her well.

Again, the difficulty of divorce requires a good support network of credentialed professionals, including a licensed mental health professional who specializes in divorce.

Research shows that people who have supportive therapy in difficult situations report feeling better more quickly than those who do not use supportive therapy. Thus, a therapist can be the key professional to help you through your divorce and after, as you rework your vision for the future. Remember, however, that therapy is a unique relationship; it could take a couple of tries to find the right fit. Don't be surprised – or give up – if your first try does not feel right.

When interviewing mental health professionals, be sure to ask what percentage of their caseload relates to people transitioning through divorce. Experience in this specific niche is critical. Often, people begin their search for a professional using search engines, but asking friends or your doctor may result in some good suggestions, too. The website psychologytoday.com is one of the largest national sites for finding therapists.

CHAPTER FOUR

Determine the Size of Your Marital Estate

Like Jane, women often find it easier to agree to settlements that seem fair without any knowledge of what they need to ensure their long-term financial security. Don't make this mistake. The harsh reality of divorcing over the age of 50 is that you have far less time to recover from a financial mistake. Depending on your age and your work experience, you may be beyond generating a significant income for yourself, making your settlement the best source of income you have. This is why doing your homework now is so critical. Regardless of the legal method you choose, it will be important to know what you need to get from a settlement to ensure your financial security.

How do you go about doing this? The starting point for any negotiation is to determine the full value of the marital estate. Many women feel totally in the dark when it comes to the finances and are reluctant to tackle money matters while in the midst of divorce. They often just want the anxiety to end and will race to the finish line without confronting the realities of their financial situations. Reasons underlying this phenomenon are complex and varied, which is why I want to now spend some time reviewing the common causes of such behavior.

Fear

Some women resist facing the reality of their financial situations because they are terrified of the outcome. In our experience, regardless of how much wealth, education, or financial savvy a woman has, her greatest fear is becoming the dreaded "bag lady." Unable to do her own analysis, this woman will accept a settlement she doesn't fully understand, relying on her husband or her attorney to take care of her.

Another possibility is that fear will paralyze a woman into inaction, to the point that the settlement may take multiple years to resolve. In my experience, the more quickly one can settle a case, the more likely the negotiations will go smoothly. This is because in the early period, following the decision to divorce, the couple often still maintains a semblance of goodwill toward one another, making negotiations more forgiving. As time wears on, these feelings ultimately diminish, making it much easier to view the negotiation as a business transaction only. Ruthlessness can ensue, ensuring an escalation of hostility that can undermine the entire negotiation process and result in years of litigation.

We therefore advise that you put your fear aside and determine to work through your financial situation, both currently and prospectively. Remember that knowledge is power, and being in the dark will only make matters worse. No matter the situation, it is far better to know now, so you can make better decisions going forward.

Consider, for example, one woman we encountered who proudly told us she had received half of the marital estate during her mediated negotiations. "It was quick and cheap," she proclaimed, "and fair." After looking over the separation agreement, it became clear that her half of the estate was made up exclusively of her husband's deferred compensation plan. While the deferred compensation did, in fact, represent half of the marital estate, this woman did not realize that deferred compensation is pre-tax money, meaning it is income that has been earned but never taxed.

The deferred compensation balance would be fully taxable to her when withdrawn, meaning that her actual settlement was equal to only 60% of what she thought she was getting. Sadly, this meant she could no longer afford her home. Meanwhile, her husband had received the after-tax assets, meaning his "half" of the marital estate was actually at least 40% more than her half. In addition to the dismal financial outcome of this case, we now had a woman who felt cheated, making it difficult to imagine an effective partnership with the father of her children.

Don't make this kind of mistake. Decide now to fully understand the value of your marital estate, your financial needs going forward, and the ramifications of any decisions you make.

Lack of Confidence

Another reason women choose to pay less attention to the finances than they should is that they lack confidence. Many of these women, especially those who have been married to highly successful men, feel inferior when it comes to financial matters. They often confuse a lack of knowledge with intellectual inferiority and are afraid of appearing incompetent. Rather than avoiding important knowledge about your marital estate, resolve to learn what you need to know. That's why we recommend making a financial advisor who specializes in divorce part of your team. This person can be your personal advocate, helping you understand all of the issues surrounding the financial side of the divorce. Once you understand the size and substance of the marital estate, as well as the tax ramifications of how an asset division might work, you will be in the driver's seat in terms of negotiating a settlement. Realize also that when women do engage financially, they are often more successful investors than their male counterparts. For example, women investors are estimated to earn average returns that are between 1% and 2% higher per year than their male counterparts. Ironically, this is because women are more likely to take professional advice and are also less reactive in the face of market volatility, opting instead to stay the course and wait for market rebounds.[5]

As a general rule, women are more thoughtful and deliberate with respect to money management and prefer a methodical, disciplined approach to investing. They will forego huge and unwarranted risk for the benefit of achieving financial security.

Desire to be the Peacemaker

In addition to feeling less knowledgeable, there is another, far more subtle barrier that may be even more dangerous for

---

[5]The Secrets of Women Investors – Kiplinger www.kiplinger.com/ .../investing/T031-C000-S002-the-secrets-of-women-investors

women. For one reason or another, they may think that simply accepting whatever makes their husbands happy is the best course for everyone.

If this feels like you, stop for a moment and ponder your motives. Perhaps you are trying to save your marriage, or to protect your children from further emotional distress. Perhaps you feel you don't deserve to share assets for which your husband has worked so hard and for so long, or perhaps you're afraid of angering him, afraid of what he might do. In a subconscious, or even conscious way, you may believe that if you "behave" during the financial settlement, the marriage will ultimately be saved or that you will actually achieve a better settlement.

In our experience, this is highly unlikely. We have yet to see a marriage reconcile at this stage of the process. Nor have we seen that asking for less results in getting more. Rather, this strategy often results in a woman receiving fewer assets and lower alimony than that to which she is entitled. Having given up her earnings power to raise a family, this woman will remain powerless in the face of inflation and her declining standard of living.

On the flip side, if you are the one who is initiating the divorce, you may feel it unfair to "take" half of the marital estate. Perhaps you feel guilty. After all, you should pay the price for ending the marriage, so the reasoning goes. Perhaps you're involved with another man and feel that your husband deserves to keep what he has earned. Perhaps you feel your new partner will take care of you.

I hate to sound clichéd, but don't deceive yourself. "A man is not a plan." You have every right to half of the marital estate, perhaps even more, depending on your circumstance.

Don't let guilt or fear of confrontation derail your financial independence. The truth is, sometimes marriages just don't work out. Women typically leave marriages after years of abuse or infidelity. You need not suffer a life of destitution just because you're finally setting yourself free.

Difficulty Quantifying the Future

Another difficulty for many women is that they simply can't envision a future for themselves. They have no idea what life will look like as a single woman. Although it's true that none of us can predict the future, you simply must force yourself to financially plan for at least two or three different scenarios.

Begin by focusing on where you will live. Would you like to be closer to your children or other relatives? Would you like to downsize from a big house into a loft apartment downtown?

Do you want to stay where you are? Perhaps you might consider one or two of these options. Next, start thinking about the things that make you happy. Who were you before you were married? Did you dream of being an artist? Traveling? Would you enjoy going back to school? Starting a new business?

Answering these questions will not only help you achieve a financial future that is acceptable to you, it will also get your mind focused on the rest of your life, rather than your past. After going through this type of process, many women come out of the divorce ready to launch into one of the options that, because of their planning, they are financially able to pursue.

Let's see what happened when Jane took the advice of the collaborative divorce attorney and decided to see a financial professional:

When I first met with the divorce financial professional, I was really nervous. I knew I couldn't answer all of her questions and worried she might say my situation was hopeless. However, as we began to talk, I immediately felt better. My advisor had worked with many divorce cases, and it was clear she knew how the process worked. She assured me that we could make the best of whatever my situation was.

This was the first time I realized that my greatest anxiety surrounding the divorce revolved around my financial security. I explained to my advisor that Bill had offered me a settlement and that I didn't want to further alienate him because I was afraid he would withdraw his offer to me or, even worse, cut me off financially. I also explained that Bill was adamant about maintaining 100% ownership of his company.

My advisor explained that we could structure a settlement in which Bill could maintain his sole ownership, but in which I could be compensated for my share of the business using other marital assets. I explained that Bill didn't have the money to buy me out and that because I was the one leaving the marriage, I didn't want to ruin his financial future.

Much to my surprise, my advisor simply said, "We're not going to worry about what Bill wants. We're going to worry about you, *what you want, and what you need, to be happy again." It may seem obvious, but this was a revelation for me. Accepting these words freed me to start building a new future for myself, shifting the focus to myself as opposed to Bill. I decided to work with my advisor to prepare a financial plan even though I was fairly confident that getting the home, half the assets outside of the business, and ample alimony for 10 years would be enough to manage my lifestyle.*

I diligently spent the time needed to review our prior bank statements and calculate our monthly expenses. With the help of my financial advisor, I also created a prospective budget for myself as a single woman. For the sake of the children, I had decided that keeping the home was in their best interest and I knew that my alimony payments would cover the cost of our monthly expenses.

After going through this process, I sat down with my advisor to look at the results. I was shocked to learn that I would be out of money in less than 10 years! I was even more surprised to learn that the "generous" alimony I was being offered was fully taxable to me, meaning that I would only get to keep about 60% of it to help pay my expenses. I couldn't begin to earn the income I would need to fill in the gap, and suddenly felt I had two really bad options: either accept Bill's offer or go head-to-head with him.

I felt backed into a corner, and that I had no choice other than to pursue a more equitable financial solution, even if it meant litigating. As difficult as this was, I was very grateful to have a more realistic idea of what it would take to support myself.

Questions to Ask

In our practice, we often work with attorneys in defining the size of the marital estate. When opaque or closely-held businesses are involved, we may additionally hire a valuations expert to help us define the value of these assets. At other times, it may be that a business was started with a modest inheritance but was ultimately grown, over the course of decades, to a significant asset. Understand that your husband's active participation in growing the business throughout the course of the marriage is a marital asset to which you have claim. These are complex situations that require work, but can dramatically change your financial outcome.

Fortunately, Jane met with a financial advisor before simply accepting Bill's offer. It then became clear to Jane that excluding the business from the marital estate – and from her settlement – was not an option. Jane's decision to pursue a more equitable distribution was the direct result of the team approach. Between her attorney, her therapist, and her financial advisor, Jane was now able to objectively evaluate her situation and her options.

The same is true for you. In order to be prepared for a fair financial negotiation, you and your team will need to answer the following questions:

- How much do I need today to ensure I can take care of myself for the rest of my life?
- How should my settlement be structured? A simple division of assets? A combination of assets and spousal support (alimony)?
- What is the tax implication of each option?
- Are there other pros and cons to consider? My ability to remarry or cohabit?
- Which option better protects me from the impact of rising costs?

By successfully answering these questions, you will find you are no longer the passive bystander, reacting only to what is being offered and settling for less than you deserve. You will instead be an active participant in your settlement, able to propose your own settlement offer, and fully confident that you understand the long-term implications of what you seek.

CHAPTER FIVE

Negotiate Your Settlement

Let's start with the basic understanding that there is only one marital estate and that, typically, when it is divided, each party is left with a lesser amount. When we talk about quantifying what your minimum acceptable settlement amount will be, we are talking about it in the context of what is available. In other words, you can't ask for a million dollars when the overall estate is worth only $750,000. Keep in mind also that the marital estate may be only a portion of your settlement. Depending on the size of your estate, the years of your marriage, and your own earnings power, you will typically also be entitled to spousal support (alimony).

With this in mind, your first step is to determine your current situation and evaluate how it will change when you are again settled following your divorce. If you're already separated, you have a leg up, because you already know what it is costing you to live independently, albeit in a temporary situation. If, however, you are still living with your husband, you will need to do some homework on developing a proposed baseline budget of your future expenses. This should, of course, include the cost of housing, utilities, and insurance. However, it should also include items such as travel, dining out, and entertainment. Remember, your life as a single woman will be different. As you contemplate the rest of your life, include costs for aspirations you may want to pursue, such as going back to school or starting a business.

Creating a budget is only part of your task. You will also need to determine the fair market value of your marital estate. As a starting point, you should gather tax returns for the past three to five years. You will also need to gather your most recent investment statements, including savings accounts and retirement accounts. These should include IRAs, 401ks, and 403b plans. Be sure you don't leave out other assets such as pension plans, whole life insurance policies, and annuities. Most importantly, don't exclude items that are difficult to value, such as closely-held businesses, partnership interests, and other illiquid investments. Even if these assets cannot be split, their value will determine what you ultimately receive by way of a settlement.

The critical next step of this process is to determine the dollar amount of assets and alimony you will need to support the lifestyle you desire. This is why looking into the future is so important. You should contemplate not just one scenario, but preferably two or three different possibilities. Remember, the minimum amount of the settlement you will need is not a guess, but the result of the goals you set. These goals are then quantified into a financial plan that includes your living expenses, your sources of income, inflation, taxes, and healthcare costs.

Additionally, your plan should contemplate the cost of long-term care insurance, if appropriate, as well as the cost of senior living. Whether you decide to age-in-place or move to a continuing-care retirement community, this expense must be included in your plan.

Once you and your financial advisor determine how much you will need, you will have to determine an appropriate structure. Keep in mind that there are multiple ways to meet your goals. For example, you may request an inequitable distribution or a lump-sum settlement in lieu of alimony. Pension survivor benefits, life insurance, and long-term care insurance can also be used to ensure financial security while providing the maximum amount of freedom for each party to move forward.

Remember, also, that as a woman you will likely live longer than your husband. This means you will require more assets to support yourself throughout your lifetime. Additionally, you've likely earned less and will have less in Social Security benefits. If you've been married at least 10 years, you're entitled to either half of your husband's Social Security benefit, referred to as a spousal benefit, or 100% of your own. This is unlike the benefit available to a widow, referred to as the survivor benefit, which is equal to 100% of your husband's benefit. Most importantly, remember that spousal support is not necessarily the best option, particularly for gray divorcers. It is generally fully-taxable to the recipient while tax-deductible to the payer. As a single taxpayer, your tax rate will be higher than when you were married, meaning you will pay more in tax on your spousal support than you might expect. Finally, remember that alimony also does not grow over time, meaning it loses purchasing power in the face of rising prices.

A good alternative to alimony might be an additional lump-sum distribution of property that equals the present value of the future alimony payments. The financial advantages of this structure are twofold: First, the additional assets received in lieu of alimony are not taxable to you, and, second, these assets can be invested to grow with inflation (and beyond), while alimony will typically remain flat, losing value over time.

A nonfinancial advantage of this structure is the freedom it affords a woman. Understand that alimony typically ceases upon cohabitation or remarriage, meaning you could find yourself choosing between love and money. In addition, your alimony could be at risk if you begin earning your own income. I've always found this factor particularly disheartening for women as it discourages them from taking ownership of their own financial lives. Instead, they opt to be fully "supported" by an ex-spouse, foregoing paths to more fulfilling lives or better standards of living.

In my view, it's far better to settle up financially upon divorce and cut the financial ties, affording yourself the freedom to pursue work, relationships, and financial independence. In spite of the lost tax deduction afforded to payers of alimony, you would be surprised by the number of men I've encountered who are eager to avoid alimony, simply to forgo the continuing burden of monthly payments.

Keep in mind too, that alimony is but one of the many considerations when contemplating an equitable distribution of assets. Because financial mistakes are so devastating for women going through gray divorce, it is important to remain wary of the following pitfalls in equitable distribution. Utilize your divorce team to unpack each of the following issues:

- Be sure you understand the difference between taxable and tax-deferred assets. A wife who believes she is getting a million dollars in deferred compensation only to learn the after-tax value is actually closer to $600,000 will be totally derailed in her financial goals.

- Be certain you devise a settlement that is tax-diverse with assets divided appropriately. Ideally, each party will have different buckets of assets from which to draw in retirement. The options are: after-tax monies, retirement assets (401k, IRA, 403b) that are typically rolled over into an IRA in your name, and Roth monies. Roth is after-tax money that has been saved into a special retirement vehicle through which earnings are never taxed.

- Also, be wary of receiving only low-basis stock in taxable accounts while your husband gets all of the high-basis stock. Low-basis stock is typically stock that has grown substantially in value, creating a large gain when sold. This will have significant tax implications and may result in an inability to liquidate your assets, or worse, huge losses in the value of the assets received, if liquidation is mandatory and the market is down.

- Understand that 401k divisions are typically distributed in cash, meaning that most plan administrators will require liquidation of assets prior to transfer of funds into your personal account. In times of market downturns, such as in 2008, this can result in substantial losses to the value of your settlement. The solution is to quickly repurchase securities at approximately the same market values, waiting until a more opportune time to liquidate. More often than not, however, we've seen such assets remain in cash, miss the market rebound and permanently impair the value of the settlement.

- Also, understand the importance of wisely investing assets for long-term growth and income. Women are particularly susceptible to fear of markets and often think it's less risky to stay in cash or CDs. Unless you have an endless supply of assets, this is a losing strategy.

- Be wary of hidden, opaque, and difficult-to-value assets, as these can often represent a significant portion of the marital estate. In the case of closely-held businesses, it is often advisable to formulate plans that enable the primary business owner to maintain full control while paying the spouse for his or her share. Depending on the value of the business, this may mean taking out a loan against the business or potentially making up the difference using other marital assets. If none of these options will work, then maintaining an ownership interest may be required. This can come in the form of stock ownership or a partnership interest, depending on how the company is structured. Whatever the case, it is strongly advised that an independent valuation of the company be obtained prior to negotiations.

- Finally, be wary of giving away too much. As previously discussed, the deep bonds unique to gray divorcers can often result in pressure to one another, as well from adult children and the extended family, to create settlements that are ultimately unsustainable. For example, a husband who has always supported his wife will now feel pressured to continue doing so, since this is the longstanding pattern of the family.

- Similarly, wives are often concerned that their husbands can't afford the divorce and are willing to leave money on the table to ensure he will be okay, especially if it is she who is initiating the divorce. Both are ever-conscious about becoming the bad guy in the eyes of the extended family.

While all this may seem like an ideal backdrop for an amicable settlement – who could ask for more conciliatory participants? – it can be surprisingly deceptive. A husband or wife suffering from a sense of loss, grief, or guilt can easily throw in the towel and agree to virtually anything, thus unbalancing the negotiation process. My colleagues and I often see situations where the husband wants to give the wife all the assets, simply to avoid paying alimony. Similarly, we've seen wives who will hand over the entire family business, because "he was the one who built it." Ultimately, both result in unsustainable settlements that will require more legal wrangling, if not continuing pressure from family members, to equalize the situation.

CHAPTER SIX

Plan *Your Financial Future*

Let's assume for a moment that you've gotten through your divorce and now have your assets in an account in your name. This might actually be the first time you're completely in charge of your own finances. If you're like most women, your focus is on asset preservation and, ultimately, long-term financial security.

Your next steps will be critical and best made with proper planning. Let's use Mary and her settlement as an example of how things might go. Like you, Mary, who is 58, is suddenly single and in charge of her own money. In addition, Mary is now also receiving alimony. She no longer has to "ask permission" every time she wants a new pair of Prada shoes! She can travel wherever she wants, whenever she wants. No questions asked.

While still suffering from the trauma of the divorce, Mary slowly begins to perceive the power she now possesses. She is *actually* in charge of her own money. After thinking this through a bit, Mary decides that she has never really liked Frank, the family financial advisor – he was, after all, truly her husband Walt's advisor. Frank never really took Mary seriously and always deferred to Walt in meetings. In fact, if Mary ever mustered up the courage to ask a question, Frank either talked down to her or talked over her, while continuing his conversation with Walt.

Mary also remembered the extreme stress of the 2008 market downturn – even Walt lost sleep over it. She couldn't imagine going through that kind of turmoil on her own, and after some deliberation, decided to fire Frank and stay in cash rather than risk her only assets in the stock market. As an added bonus, Mary reasoned, she would no longer have to pay investment management fees.

Mary contemplated her situation carefully. She had received a million dollars in assets as part of her settlement. In addition, she had received 100% of the family home, valued at $500,000, with no mortgage. From her pre-divorce planning, Mary knew she spent only $70,000 per year, and that a full $60,000 of it would come from alimony until her age 66, at which point, she would receive half of her ex-husband's social security, equaling $20,000 per year.

This meant that Mary would only be withdrawing $10,000 per year until her age 66, and then $50,000 per year from then on. Using simple math, Mary calculated this money should last about 26 years. (She would withdraw $10,000 per year for eight years and then $50,000 per year for another 18 years before running out of money.) Mary would be 84 years old by then – and reasoned she would have enough money to take care of herself over her lifetime, with no stock market risk.

On the surface, this all sounds well and good. Unfortunately, it's simply wrong. Mary has not contemplated the income taxes that will be due on the alimony she receives, or the income taxes that will be due on the portion of her assets that are in retirement accounts. While it's true that Mary received $1 million as part of her settlement, only $300,000 of it was in after-tax assets. The remaining balance of $700,000 came to her in an individual retirement account (IRA). Because IRA monies have never been taxed, they become fully taxable when withdrawn.

More importantly, Mary has not considered the powerful impact of inflation. Remember how cheap things were when you were a child? I remember that my parents purchased their first home for $24,000 when I was nine years old. Today, one can hardly buy a car for that amount of money.

Generally speaking, if we assume the average long-term rate of inflation is 3%, you will experience a 50% reduction of purchasing power every 24 years, even with no increase in spending at all. In short, while your dollars may look the same, they buy much less. Inflation is the primary reason people invest in the financial markets – so their assets will continue to keep pace with price increases.

As Illustration 1 on the following page demonstrates, Mary will run out of money in a short 14 years if she stays in cash. Again, her personal spending, her income taxes, and rising prices due to inflation simply wear down her assets to nothing by the time Mary is just 72 years old. This is a full 12 years sooner than she had expected.

Fortunately, for our purposes, Mary is a fictional character. Unlike the rest of us, she gets a "do over." Let's see what happens if Mary decides to invest her assets in a conservative, balanced portfolio comprised of 60% stocks and 40% fixed income.

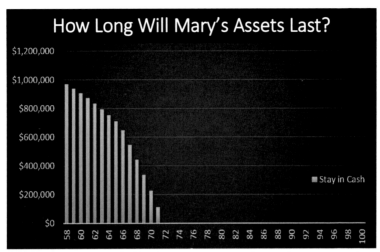

Illustration 1: Mary holds $1,000,000 in cash. Cash is assumed to generate no return.

Using the same long-term inflation rate of 3% but offsetting it with a long-term, average investment return of 7% per year, we can see in Illustration 2 below that Mary's assets now last almost twice as long, to age 85.

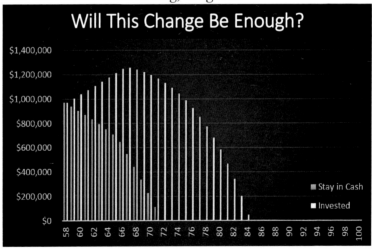

Illustration 2: Mary invests $1,000,000 in a balanced portfolio. Cash is assumed to generate no return.

Mary is happier with this outcome but still concerned because, like her mother and grandmother, she hopes to live beyond age 85. What else can Mary do? She can either increase her earnings or reduce her spending. After considering several options, including downsizing or going back to work, Mary decides that by the time she's 75 she would like to consider a move into a continuing-care retirement community (CCRC). Mary is not unusual in this – even though the national average age of entry to a CCRC is 80,[6] we find that many single women prefer to move in earlier, since the move provides them with an immediate sense of community, friendship and even romantic options.

For planning purposes, we conservatively assume that Mary sells her home and after paying all fees, receives $500,000 at her age 75. We then assume Mary pays an entrance fee of $250,000 to a CCRC and deposits the remaining proceeds of $250,000 from the sale of her home into her investment portfolio.

Because Mary feels she will likely stop buying Prada shoes by age 75, she also plans to reduce her spending by $1,500 per month. This will not be difficult for Mary, since the move to a retirement community eliminates the expensive upkeep and maintenance of her home, including the property taxes, lawn care and the endless appliance and home repairs. In addition, some of Mary's food and entertainment expenses are covered as part of her new retirement lifestyle.

---

[6]A. Ebeling, September 26, 2011, Continuing Care Communities: A Big Investment with Catches, *Forbes*.

As Illustration 3 shows, making these changes extends Mary's portfolio beyond her age 100, a full 28 years longer than her initial plan of staying in cash. Accordingly, Mary is now in a position to purchase the long-term care insurance she wants, which will help lessen the risk of plan failure if she has a health event requiring assisted living or skilled nursing.

Illustration 3: At age 75 Mary adds $250,000 to her investments and reduces her spending by $1,500 per month. Cash is assumed to generate no return.

Mary is pleased to know that her planning will ensure she doesn't run out of money in her lifetime. She knows that so long as she follows the parameters of the plan, she will be okay.

This doesn't mean, of course, that Mary won't have life events that interrupt her plan. For example, what if Mary decides to remarry? What if she has a health event? Again, these are all things we plan for as they arise.

CHAPTER SEVEN

Follow Your Instincts and Invest Like a Girl!

Now that you have a financial plan for your financial future, it's important to implement it. Your first order of business will be to learn to trust your instincts. This is because women are actually known to be better investors than men! (More on that below – keep reading.) Unless you have the interest, knowledge and desire to manage your own investments, your next step will be to find a financial advisor you trust – one who understands your unique, feminine investing temperament. Studies have shown repeatedly that women are different kinds of investors than men. Generally, women have a more measured investment approach, are less inclined to overconfidence, therefore, less reactive to market changes, consequently achieving better results. And unlike men, women generally want a more holistic relationship with their advisor, seeking to be understood in more ways than just their pocketbooks.[7]

For most women, finding an advisor who understands their values and life goals – someone who really "gets" who

---

[7]The Secrets of Women Investors – Kiplinger www.kiplinger.com/ .../investing/T031-C000-S002-the-secrets-of-women-investors

they are – is the most critical part of the equation. Sadly, in a still male-dominated industry, women are often ridiculed for their more naturally conservative approach to investing, either talked down to or dismissed entirely by advisors who expect buy-in of investment strategies that just don't "feel" right. In fact, while many of today's financial firms claim to "hear" women's unique perspectives, they continually offer the same investment strategies for women as for their male clients, essentially doing nothing more than changing the font to pink in their marketing materials. This is unfortunate when you consider that women investors actually out-earn their male counterparts by as much as 1% to 2% per year.[8]

According to Louann Lofton (author of *Warren Buffett Invests Like a Girl: And Why You Should, Too,* HarperCollins, 2011), women are more cautious, take fewer risks, are less susceptible to peer pressure, do more research, and are ultimately more patient investors. Although some in the industry claim that women are "scared," research shows instead that men are overconfident investors who will generally take more risk and follow a herd-like mentality, trading more often and ultimately dragging down their investment returns.

While part of long-term investment success includes finding someone with whom you personally connect, the other part is finding a firm that is mutually aligned with your investment success. As you'll see below, not all firms are created equal in this respect. In fact, the financial services industry has very effectively blurred the distinctions between

---

[8]The Secrets of Women Investors – Kiplinger www.kiplinger.com/
.../investing/T031-C000-S002-the-secrets-of-women-investors

the different pricing models found in the industry. As an investor, your number one goal is to find someone who can offer you objective advice with the most amount of transparency and the least amount of self-interest when advising you. Take the time to review and understand each of the models below before making any decisions about your future advisor. The financial model of the firm you are contemplating should be a key factor in your decision-making process.

Broker/Dealer Model

Remember the old stereotype of the rich investor smoking a cigar by the pool? He would invariably receive an urgent call from his broker with a "hot" stock tip. The investor would ask a couple of questions, give the green light to buy, and ultimately set off a flurry of trading activity.

Long gone are the days of manual trading, but the broker model is alive and well. Although electronic trading has revolutionized the industry, the compensation structure of this model remains virtually unchanged. Brokers are still paid a commission based on the number and dollar values of the trades they place. Only now, they can additionally be compensated by the actual funds they purchase for you. Sales loads, kickbacks, and a portion of the fund's annual expense ratio are all potential forms of compensation that go to the broker. Unfortunately, many of these fees are hidden and/or require additional investigation, making it difficult, if not impossible, to know exactly what you are paying for investment management. Instead, these hidden fees simply reduce the net returns you see on your statement.

In addition, because the broker is often incentivized to sell a particular security by the issuing company, it's difficult to know whether the investment is actually the best one for you or for your broker. While a broker may have the best of intentions, the typical broker/dealer compensation structure inherently creates a conflict of interest. It's only natural that even the most honest broker would prefer to sell a product that pays him more. And since, as a consumer, you can't distinguish the difference, it's probably best to avoid this model. Furthermore, excessive trading costs, hidden fees, and a potential lack of objectivity can substantially impair your investment returns over the long term.

Understand also that a broker has an allegiance to his own firm that may compromise his ability to put his clients' interests first. While legislation may be changing, brokers are just obligated to ensure that a recommended investment is suitable for a specific client, and do not have a fiduciary responsibility to always act in their clients' best interest. He/she is compensated the same regardless of whether your investments make money or not – again, based on commissions. In addition, brokers often work for large financial institutions that offer a myriad of other services. As a client, this will make you vulnerable to significant cross-selling. Don't be surprised if you receive offers to refinance your mortgage, expand your home-equity loan, purchase long-term-care insurance, or "invest" in an annuity, all of which will ultimately benefit not only the financial institution, but your broker. The broker/dealer segment of the industry has done a remarkably good job of keeping its compensation structure quiet, but savvy investors ultimately have demanded more transparency, leading to the fee-only model.

Fee-Only Model

The fee-only model is considered by many objective sources to be the most transparent structure – and the one most mutually aligned with the investor. First and foremost, Registered Investment Advisors (RIAs) who subscribe to the fee-only model are fiduciaries, taking an oath to put their clients' interests ahead of their own. In addition, their fees are affected directly by their performance as asset managers. Because fee-only firms charge based on a percentage of assets under management, their fees go up as your investments increase. Likewise, their fees decline as your investments decline, putting you squarely on the same side of the table.

Most importantly, advisory fees are much more transparent in the fee-only model and the advisor has no financial incentive to place you in an investment that may not be in your best interest. In addition, because these independent registered advisors are not affiliated with banks or wire houses, they do not have their own products to sell. Rather than trying to sell you a mutual fund offered by his or her own bank, a fee-only advisor will select your investments from the universe of available funds, making those selections based on the investment's merits rather than on what they get paid. Remember, these advisors are compensated based on your asset value, not on the number of transactions or the funds they place you in.

This model is particularly well-suited for women who prefer a more disciplined approach, with no incentives for trading more.

Fee-Based Model

Be especially wary of a fee-*based* model, which can often confuse investors given the similarity of its name to the fee-*only* model. The fee-based model combines the brokerage model and the fee-only model, meaning you will pay fees based on a percentage of assets under management, but could also pay commissions depending on the products sold. Many in the industry consider this the most expensive of all models.

New Standards Toward Protecting Consumers

Unsurprisingly, a battle has been waging for some time between the commission/fee-based Wall Street firms and the independent fee-only advisory community over the need to expand the **fiduciary standard** so that *all* advisors, regardless of business model, are required to put the investor's interests ahead of their own. Consequently, the U.S. Department of Labor recently issued a new ruling (effective as of April 10, 2017), forcing all advisors to act as fiduciaries when advising investors on their *retirement assets*. Note: this ruling *does not apply* to non-retirement assets, including any after-tax savings and investments, proceeds resulting from the sale of your home, alimony or other after-tax assets received from your divorce settlement.

The new **U.S. Department of Labor Conflict of Interest Final Rule** is a good step forward in better consumer protection for your IRA and retirement plan assets. Now all of the various financial service firms and practitioners will need to adhere to the five key criteria that consumers say they want in a planner or advisor. These include *integrity, objectivity, loyalty, knowledge* and *expertise.* The new "Best Interests" standard requires firms to adopt anti-conflict policies and better police its advisors. Obviously, Wall Street firms and many insurance companies and banks would prefer to continue selling products, even if it isn't the best option for the consumer. It will be interesting to see how the broker/dealers adapt their policies and culture to meet the new fiduciary standard.

While there are still some holes in the new legislation, this new ruling is a strong step in the right direction. When dealing with a Wall Street brokerage firm, big bank, or insurance company with your retirement assets, keep an eye towards new disclosures they will be required to send you in 2017. They may provide clues as to how consumer-friendly your advisor really is. And don't forget: these new standards don't apply to your non-retirement plan assets.

Mary

After being in the dark for a long time, I decided once and for all that I would learn enough about investing to know when I'm being dealt with fairly and when I'm not. It turns out that common sense was my best guide when it came to choosing an investment advisor and understanding how my goals and my investments synced up with one another.

My checklist for choosing my advisor included the following:

- Does the firm have a good reputation? *I asked my friends, my CPA, and my attorney, "What investment advisors would you recommend who are honest and ethical and won't talk over my head or try to sell me products I don't want or need?" Turns out this was a short list.*

- Does this firm work with people like me? *As I met with the advisors on the short list, I found that some were more interested in bigger fish than me, some were late in their professional lives with no clear succession plans, and some just didn't understand (or want to understand) my unique problems. I was tired of being talked down to or talked over, and I wanted someone who truly respected my thoughts. I didn't want to be viewed as "less than" because I was a woman.*

- Is this a fee-only firm? *I had read an article about the growth of true fee-only advisors, as opposed to the ones getting paid by commission for selling an annuity (which my bank "advisor" tried to do!) or life-insurance product, or using some vague "fee-based" term. "Fee-only" means an advisor gets no hidden compensation and acts as a true fiduciary, looking out for my best interest above his or her own. It also turns out many advisors are considered "agents," which means their allegiance is to their company instead of to their client.*

- Does the firm outsource all of its research, or does it have an in-house team that understands investment markets and can shift quickly as markets change? *This was yet another "aha" moment for me — financial advisors have extremely varied backgrounds, and many are better at selling than actually understanding what it is they are selling. Many of the ones I interviewed weren't very creative: They put their clients into a static bucket of investments and then paid minimal attention to the changing economic landscape or to their clients' changing situations.*

- Are the employees of the firm well-credentialed? *I learned enough to know that I wanted my firm to have several designations and disciplines represented, including the CFA® or Chartered Financial Analyst® designation, which is the highest designation in* the investment industry. *CFA® charterholders are trained to do more research and to fully understand portfolio construction. Having a CFA® charterholder as part of your team, in collaboration with other professionals who have achieved the CPA, CFP® or CDPA designations can certainly be a plus in helping you receive qualified and objective advice.*

- Does the firm offer financial planning? *Another revelation – it's hard to know what the right investment mix is without understanding what I'll need at various stages of my life. I found that for me, the most powerful approach to meeting my goals was to have a good financial plan that informed my investment strategy. I also wanted ongoing monitoring to make sure I was moving towards my desired goals.*

- Are the fees reasonable? *Generally, being charged fees above 1% for investment management and regular consulting creates too much of a drag on investment returns. I learned quickly that some of the big mutual-fund companies that stress low fees as their number-one differentiator were the very ones who were selling their own products, with little to no regard for what would be best for my portfolio – another reason the fee-only advisor made sense to me. I decided I would rather pay a transparent, flat fee for investment management than get into a "low-cost" situation where my fees were hidden or where the advisor was incentivized to "sell" me a product.*

Before moving forward with any investment plan, be certain to find the right fee structure. We recommend a fiduciary relationship that will ensure the greatest transparency and objectivity in your investment management.

CHAPTER EIGHT

Fundamentals of Investing

Regardless of what firm you select or who ultimately becomes your financial advisor, it is important to educate yourself on the basic concepts surrounding investing. You will want to know enough to understand *how* your money is being invested and *why*. Most importantly, you will want to know enough to confidently describe your natural investment temperament and risk tolerance. For this reason, we've devoted an entire chapter to the fundamentals of investing. Take time to read this section and to understand its contents before proceeding with any investment plan.

Investment Options

There are essentially three traditional places to invest your assets: cash, bonds, and stocks. Many of the world's greatest investors still use these three areas for the bulk of their investment assets.

Cash. Cash is the term used to refer to money in your checking or savings account, certificates of deposit (CDs), and money-market funds. Although it may be tempting to hold large amounts of cash, remember that there have been very few periods over the past 100 years that cash has earned enough interest to keep up with rising costs. For this reason, having too much cash on hand can be dangerous to your ability to maintain your lifestyle over the long-term.

Still, it's important to have enough cash on hand to meet needs arising from unexpected events, such as health issues or home repairs. You may consider holding even more cash if you don't have a steady stream of income from sources such as a pension, alimony, or social security. This is important, because it will prevent you from having to sell investments during inopportune times, such as during the 2008 market downturn. It's always better to wait for the market to recover rather than to sell assets when markets are down. In addition, holding cash will prevent you from incurring unnecessary trading costs every time you need a little help with your monthly budget. As discussed above, excessive trading over long periods of time can significantly impair your overall investment returns.

Bonds. A bond essentially represents a loan you make to a third party, such as a company, for a pre-defined period of time. In exchange for the loan, you will typically receive periodic interest payments during the life of the loan – and ultimately, at maturity, you will receive your original investment (loan amount) back. Bonds can be issued by private or public companies and can also include the U.S. Government.

Government bonds are typically defined by length of time. For example, Treasury bills (T-bills) are typically issued for a period of one year or less. Treasury notes are typically issued for periods of three, five, or 10 years, and Treasury bonds are issued for periods of more than 10 years. You can also loan money to state governments and receive tax-free income (i.e. exempt from federal taxes and potentially state taxes as well depending on your state of residence) – an especially attractive feature for those in higher tax brackets.

Bonds can be held individually or as part of a diversified portfolio of multiple bonds in the form of a mutual fund or an exchange-traded fund (ETF). Each of these funds can own a mix of municipal tax-free bonds, corporate bonds, and government bonds depending on their specific investment mandate.

Investors generally take great comfort in knowing they will receive their initial investment, referred to as the *par* value or *principal* value, at maturity, in addition to the periodic interest payments received throughout the term of the bond's life. Of course, the bond issuer's ability to repay this amount will depend on its credit quality.

High-quality bonds are backed by financially strong issuers and provide more assurance to investors, as compared to lower-quality bonds, with regard to the issuer's ability to pay the bond's interest and principal in a timely manner. Lower-quality bond issuers typically have to pay higher interest rates to compensate investors for the additional uncertainty related to their ability to pay on a timely basis – or at all. Fortunately, there are independent rating services that provide bond ratings to indicate the bond issuer's credit quality.

Historically, investors have relied on bond interest to provide them with regular income during retirement. Unfortunately, the current low interest rate environment has left many investors wondering why they should invest in bonds at all. Not only are coupon rates low, but as interest rates inevitably rise, the value of the underlying bonds decline, meaning that selling the bonds before maturity will result in a loss of principal.

The reason to invest in bonds in today's environment can be explained simply: Bonds provide an excellent shock absorber to stock-market volatility. During the Great Recession of 2008, many high-quality bonds, particularly U.S. government-related debt, went *up* over 7% while stock prices plummeted as much as 50%. Because many bonds have income-producing and asset-preservation qualities, we feel bonds are an important component of any portfolio, particularly those funding retirement. Investors in retirement should have varying mixes of maturities and types of bonds, designed to work with their financial goals and plans.

Stocks. As risky as the stock market may seem, it's important to note that the stock market has been the greatest generator of wealth in this country, having returned an average annual rate of close to 10% since 1926. With that said, stocks are volatile and need to be held for longer time periods in order to approach their long-term historical averages.

For many women, stock markets feel "random," often rising and falling for no apparent reason. However, stocks represent actual ownership interests in real companies that trade on public stock-market exchanges. Although it's true that short-term stock prices, often driven by consumer sentiment, are volatile, it's also true that over a three- to five-year period, stock prices are much more predictable, as they are more closely aligned with the underlying values of the companies they represent. For this reason, we generally advise that stocks or stock funds be owned for a minimum holding period of three to five years.

Stocks can be owned in a variety of ways, including outright (usually in a custodial account), in mutual funds (creating better diversification), or exchange-traded funds (essentially a hybrid of a mutual fund that trades on a stock exchange). Each of these ownership forms have pros and cons that will be important to understand as you and your advisor develop your investment plan.

Remember, however, that assets needed in the short-term to fund your expenses should not be invested in the stock market, but rather held in either cash or money market, where their future values are more predictable.

Asset Allocation and Diversification

Asset allocation is the term used to describe how much of your assets are invested in each of the various investment options (i.e. major asset classes) outlined above – stocks, bonds, and cash. The way your assets are allocated to the available options is likely *the* most important component of your investment strategy. In fact, studies show that as much as *90%* of investment success is dependent on asset allocation – *not* on the particular stocks one holds.[9] This is because, historically, the returns of the three major asset classes have not moved together.

Because the major asset classes do not move up and down together, and because no one can predict with any degree of accuracy which asset class will perform better in any given year, having a diversified portfolio that includes an allocation to stocks, to bonds, and to cash will not only reduce the overall

[9]Setting the Record Straight on Asset Allocation - CFA Institute Blogs https://blogs.cfainstitute.org/investor/.../setting-the-record-straight-on-asset-allocation

volatility within your portfolio, but will also allow you to take advantage of higher-return investments such as stocks, while protecting some of your money in less volatile investments such as cash and bonds. Note that diversifying *within* each asset class is also important and will further reduce risk in the portfolio. (See Appendix A: Historical Asset Class Performance.)

How much you should have allocated to each asset class depends on the time horizon of your cash needs and your overall willingness (and ability) to bear risk. Your financial advisor should be able to help you determine some of these factors, but only with your input. For example, now that you're single again, you may want to move, go back to school, start a new business, or travel. It's very difficult to know the implications of these decisions on the longevity of your investment portfolio. For this reason, we recommend multi-scenario financial planning to help clients determine not only the viability of their various goals, but the right mix of investments to help them achieve those goals.

We generally prefer not to use investing rules of thumb, simply because such rules often don't account for individual circumstances. With that said, the following guidelines can generally be followed in the absence of a financial plan. If you have a major cash need approaching and your time horizon is:

- One to three years away, consider putting more of these funds into cash investments;
- Three to five years away, consider a mix of cash, stocks, and bonds;

- Five to ten years away or more, consider investing more in stocks (but usually not solely), assuming this aligns with your desired risk tolerance.

For higher net-worth investors, other good options are available. (See Appendix B: Understanding Alternative Investments.)

Investment Risk

We women face a particularly difficult conundrum when it comes to investing. On the one hand, our tendency toward risk-aversion can make us fearful of financial markets. On the other hand, our longer life expectancies require an investment strategy that will support our cash needs, while also keeping up with inflation. For this reason, most of us recognize that investing our assets is essential for long-term financial security. The goal is therefore to define an appropriate level of risk for our individual situations.

Let's take a moment now to understand the various risks involved:

Purchasing Power Risk, otherwise known as *inflation risk*, is the danger that our money will not buy as much in the future as it does today. This occurs because over time, inflation increases the cost of the goods and services we buy. If we're unable to grow our assets to keep pace with rising costs, we either end up lowering our standard of living, or we end up spending a little more of our nest egg each year, until ultimately, we run out of money. In most cases, we end up doing both.

In recent decades, inflation has been relatively tame, averaging 2% to 3% per year, or even less. Even modest inflation, however, is like death by a thousand cuts. Let's look at the last 10 years for a real-life example. During this period, prices have increased by 20%. This means that today you are actually able to buy 20% fewer goods and services than you could just a decade ago, with the same amount of money. In practical terms, this is no different from making a bad investment and losing 20% of its value.

The loss of purchasing power is the very real risk of staying in cash. To illustrate this risk, let's now revisit what happens to Mary when she decides to stay in cash. Sadly, she runs out of money in fewer than 14 years. Remember, not investing at all, or investing too conservatively, is one of *the* biggest threats to your long-term financial security.

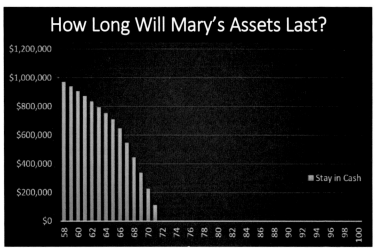

Illustration 1: Mary holds $1,000,000 in cash. Cash is assumed to generate no return.

Loss of Principal is the primary reason most women are wary of financial markets. It may be tempting to put your cash settlement into a savings account or into a Certificate of

Deposit (CD), because you know that your principal will be safe. It's true that you won't lose your principal, but once again, you will subject yourself to the purchasing power risk described above. This will mean either dramatically reducing your lifestyle or running out of money.

Again, the best way to protect your principal is to diversify your portfolio among the various asset classes while maintaining a disciplined, consistent approach. This is often easier said than done because of the volatility of the financial markets.

Many conservative investors find the stock market unsettling because of its inherent daily and weekly fluctuations in value. It's true that on average, the stock market has declined 14.2% per year from peak to trough during the last 37 years (see chart below). What this tells us is that stock market volatility is a normal part of investing and is something that has to be accepted in order to maintain purchasing power. It's important to note from the chart on the following page that in 28 of the last 37 years, the stock market has ended the year higher than it started.

Consequently, diversifying your portfolio with an appropriate asset allocation is the best way to mitigate the full brunt of stock-market volatility because as one asset class goes down, another will typically go up, thereby reducing (not eliminating) the overall fluctuations in your portfolio. Ultimately, however, you will need to accept that your portfolio will rise and fall with the market. Remember, stock market volatility will only harm you if you have to sell stocks when they are down to cover expenses (hence the need for reasonable cash reserves) or you panic and sell at the bottom and don't get back in until stock prices are much higher.

S&P 500 intra-year declines vs. calendar year returns
Despite average intra-year drops of 14.2%, annual returns positive in 28 of 37 years

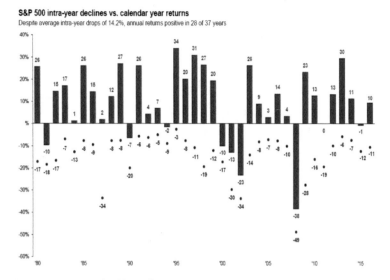

Source: FactSet, Standard & Poor's, J.P. Morgan Management.
Returns are based on price index only and do not include dividends. Intra-year drops refers to the largest market drops from a peak to a trough during the year. For illustrative purposes only. Returns shown are calendar year returns from 1980 to 2016.
J.P. Morgan Asset Management *Guide to the Markets – U.S.* Data are as of December 31, 2016.

> "Be fearful when others are greedy
> and greedy when others are fearful."
> — *Warren Buffett*

This may sound easy, but it's not. The 24/7 media incessantly telling us how bad things are, can tempt even the strongest investors to sell at the bottom of the market – at exactly the wrong time. While market bottoms are only known in hindsight, if you do end up selling at or near the bottom of the market, you are turning *a temporary, unrealized loss into a permanent one that will be virtually impossible to regain.* In fact, buying "high" and selling "low" is the primary reason the average investor has earned less than 3% over the last 20 years, rather than the 6% to 8% she could have earned over the same time period by sticking with a diversified investment strategy.[10]

If you're having an anxiety attack, take some deep breaths, talk to your financial advisor, and remember that a disciplined, consistent approach has proven over time to be the best way to achieve investment success. Fortunately, that's the way most women prefer to invest naturally.

If you find you're simply unable to tune out the noise and anxiety of market volatility, then you may want to consider lowering your allocation to stocks a bit and replacing them with "safer" investments such as bonds. Lowering your stock exposure radically should be done only in extreme circumstances.

Sequencing Risk. Assuming you need to supplement your other sources of income, such as social security or alimony, with withdrawals from your portfolio, you will need to ensure that your portfolio is generating a reasonable amount of income. Today's low-interest-rate environment has made this exceedingly difficult.

As such, most investors are now focused on overall return, which includes both income and asset appreciation. Note that both the income generated by your portfolio, and the growth of your portfolio due to rising market values, generate cash you can use without impairing your principal, regardless of market conditions. Withdrawing these amounts will leave your original

---

[10]Source: Dalbar Inc., 12/31/15

nest egg intact, so that it can continue producing income and generating gains over the long term. But what happens if the market is down and your withdrawals exceed both the income and appreciation in your portfolio? This results in an erosion of principal, which is very difficult to overcome.

The chart on the following page illustrates the impact of withdrawing assets when markets are down. Both the investor represented on the left (retirement scenario #1) and the investor on the right (retirement scenario #2) have one million dollars in assets. Each investor withdraws $50,000 (or 5% of the initial $1 million) per year for a 20-year period. Let's see how varying market conditions impact these two investors.

Investor #1 begins withdrawing during a normal market cycle and continues this pattern for 16 years. In years 17 to 20, however, the market begins to drop until it declines a total of 20%. Investor #1 continues his normal annual withdrawals and, in spite of the market downturn, is still left with $1.7 million dollars in year 20.

Let's now look at investor #2. She also starts with a million dollars and withdraws $50,000 per year for 20 years. However, in her case, the market dips 20% in years 1 to 3. Sadly, due to nothing more than bad timing, this investor runs out of money in year 19.

There are several ways to avoid this outcome. One is to hold enough cash reserves to cover a market downturn, so that no assets are being sold during this period. A $150,000 cash reserve ($50,000 per year for three years) would have prevented investor #2 from spending down assets during a market downturn – avoiding a disastrous result.

Retirement Scenario #1

Account returns 7% annually on average
(positive investment returns in the first years)

Account returns

Retirement Scenario #2

Account returns 7% annually on average
(negative investment returns in the first years)

Account returns

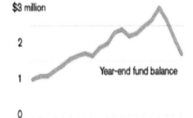

Retiree #1 has $1.7 million left over after 20 years...

Year-end fund balance

...Retiree #2 runs out of money.

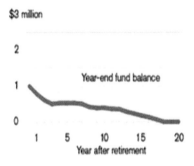

Year-end fund balance

Retirees make identical withdrawals...

Annual withdrawals by retiree #1

...until year 19, when retiree #2 runs out of money.

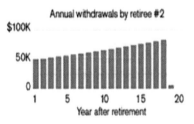

Annual withdrawals by retiree #2

Source: Russell Investments.

Another way to reduce the sequencing risk is to ensure that there are enough income-producing assets in the portfolio to cover your fixed expenses. These include dividend-paying stocks, interest-paying bonds, and annuities, when appropriate. Remember, income generated by your portfolio works just like cash and can be withdrawn without impairing principal, regardless of market conditions.

An additional way to produce income from your portfolio, particularly in our current low- interest-rate environment, is to allocate a portion of your holdings to "alternative" investments that are less correlated with traditional stock and bond markets (see Appendix B). These come in a variety of flavors and include such investments as income-producing real estate properties, private equity, or middle-market lending. Be wary, however, as these can be more risky and less liquid than the traditional asset classes and require professional vetting by your advisory firm. Due to these additional risk considerations, some private alternative investments, deemed private placements, are only available to accredited investors, who meet specific income or net worth thresholds.

Behavioral Finance Risk. Finally – and this is a big one – is the risk of making investment decisions based on emotions such as fear or greed. It's easy enough to understand the desire to buy into the market when it's going gang busters – and to sell out of the market when it's plummeting. What this amounts to, however, is something none of us wants to do – that is, to "buy high and sell low."

This behavior can completely derail your investment success and is among the primary reasons the average investor has earned less than inflation during the past 20 years when she should have earned somewhere between 6% to 8% per year (depending on asset allocation). A good financial education, along with an advisor you trust, will be your best defense against making an emotional decision at exactly the wrong time.

Judy

My number-one risk is a portfolio that isn't growing over time. I'm only 60 years old and have at least two decades to travel, to share experiences with my children and grandchildren, and to explore different "encore" hobbies and activities.

I want at least nine months of living expenses kept in cash at all times. If my advisor believes risks are heightened in general or in my portfolio, I'm willing to go up to two to three years of cash.

I'm willing to explore a few more aggressive investment options, but no more than 10% of my overall portfolio.

I'd like to stay in high-quality assets with at least 70% of my portfolio. My view after considerable research is the higher the quality, the better the chance an investment will bounce back over a five-year period of time if we have a major crash, recession, or other unexpected shock to the economy.

CHAPTER NINE

Move Beyond Your Divorce

Although there is no universal path toward healing, there is at least one universal theme that is mandatory: resilience. I didn't really understand this concept until shortly after my separation, when I escaped to Italy to study painting. Landing in a country to which I had never been, alone, unable to speak Italian, and nursing my broken heart, I made my way to the three-story flat in which I would spend the better part of the summer. I was greeted by three women who would share this place with me, both physically and rhetorically. I was surprised to learn we were all similarly in transition, with two of us recently separated, one recently widowed, and one on the cusp of retirement – all of us in pursuit of an unknown, and a sense of purpose and meaning. Sharing the secrets of our lives with one another was easy, as we were, in a way, anonymous to one another's worlds. Our hopes and dreams, our heartaches, our losses, all flowed with the Italian wine accompanying every meal. During the weeks ahead, we worked hard, ate well, explored, shopped, and painted, except for Colette who was enrolled in the sculpting program.

Colette was a very attractive 70-year-old, with platinum blond hair, skinny jeans, and a positively modern mentality. Sadly, she had recently lost her husband to cancer, her mother to old age, her daughter to suicide, and her brother to a heart attack – all of this within the last four years. Yet here she was, in a foreign country, decades older than the rest of us, honing her craft, contemplating a three-year, full-time program.

I reveled in Colette's apparent well-being and longed for her secret. One night over a glass of wine, I expressed my amazement at her resilience. "Colette, I want to be you when I grow up. How is it that I'm a basket case after one lousy divorce, and you're thriving after having lost four loved ones in just four years?" She proceeded to tell us all the story of an outward-bound-type experience she had had in upstate New York when in her early 30s.

"We were made to stay up all through the night, and then solve complex problems the next day," she said. "We even had to perform mind over matter, walking on hot coals without flinching. But nothing impacted me like the paint-ball game of the last night."

Apparently, the paint-ball game was brutal. In the dark of the night, on a large field, each person had to shoot others or be shot. The rules of the game were that if you were shot, you were not allowed to leave the field. Rather, you had to go to the sidelines, lie on the ground, and play dead. Colette described the pain of being shot, the screams suggestive of real combat. About 20 minutes into the game, after being shot, she appreciatively made her way to the sidelines, lying down and playing dead. She continued to hear the sounds of combat in the night sky and was relieved and elated to be out of the game – at first.

As she lay there, contemplating her defeat, Colette began to consider what she could have done differently. Having been shot, she was no longer a rookie and, suddenly, she had a strong desire to get back onto the field and play, this time for a win. "I wanted to be relevant again, to be back where the action was."

Colette went on to explain that this singular lesson was one she would apply to the rest of her life. From that moment forward, Colette expected to be "shot down" in life but, recalling the cold, dark field in upstate New York, she also knew she would always "get back in the game. The sooner you start, the more you will live."

I liked the sound of this, because I knew I too wanted to "live" again. I began to embrace my pain as an integral part of my life, honoring my grief while embarking on a path out of the darkness. Standing outside of myself, I realized that every decision I would make would shape what my future would be. I had two choices: Either indulge in self-pity and bitterness or accept that this transition would be a necessary gateway to something better, more exciting, and ultimately, more sustainable.

I chose the latter, and while not easy, I can honestly say I've had more love, more personal connection, more poignancy, and more accomplishment in the last seven years than my entire married life. My children and I suffered, but we also thrived. We became bound together in our adversity, each of us caring for the other, in silence. Until one day, seemingly without rhyme or reason, the sun shone again.

In my work I've had the privilege of collaborating not only with divorcing women, but also with the women who would emerge out of that chaos into brand new lives, designed by and for the stronger, wiser, and more independent women they became. Although the details of your specific journey won't be exactly the same as theirs, your striving to achieve the following milestones will ensure your own healthy recovery and, ultimately, a new life for the new you.

Honor Your Pain

If you're in the midst of a divorce negotiation, you are likely in survival mode, doing nothing more than reacting to the legal, financial, and practical issues surrounding your situation. However, buried beneath the immediate and practical considerations of your divorce, there is the realization of a failed dream. None of us married in our youth expecting to end things like this.

The end of the marriage signals not only the end of the "dream," but the end of the long-standing family unit and all that went with it. It is a significant loss, and one that must be honored.

During this period, you may feel angry, sad, hurt, and even despondent. I recall that certain situations and conversations only seemed to make it worse. Well-intentioned friends would speak of seeing my husband, who appeared to have moved on with his life. Others would comment about how sad my children seemed. Various members of the extended family were happy to lay blame. All of this only added to the stress of the situation, making it more difficult to bear. This is when a good friend offered me advice. "Draw a circle around yourself," she said, "and don't let anyone inside who is not completely supportive, empathetic, and loving toward you." I realized how important this was and followed her advice. And it helped, because this was the most difficult period of the entire process.

Care for Yourself

It's easy during this highly emotional time to inadvertently stop caring for yourself. You may not realize that you are slipping out of your normal habits, perhaps sleeping more or less or eating more or less. More than ever before, you must make it a priority to consciously take care of yourself. Start by getting a physical. Share your situation with your doctor, so all are on alert as to the stressful period you're in. A good therapist is essential. Find someone to whom you can talk freely and openly. In spite of your well-meaning friends and family, most are utterly untrained in helping you emotionally. No matter how hard, make time for exercise, even if only a short walk each day. Yoga can be a good way to calm your body and your mind.

Learn from Your Prior Relationship

Something went terribly wrong in your marriage. Although it may be easy to blame it all on your husband, remember that the relationship itself was the root of the problem – a relationship in which you participated. Time and again, people repeat the patterns of their old relationships, ending up with the same devastating outcomes. Since I know you never want to be here again, it's critical to now take stock of what went wrong. Did you assume the role of the parent or child in the relationship? Often, such power imbalances are unsustainable, with the "parent" becoming tired of carrying the load, or the "child" becoming tired of having no voice.

Both cause resentment.

Another common issue leading to the end of a relationship is an inability to communicate effectively. Was this true in your marriage?

These are not questions that can be answered easily, but taking the time to evaluate your relationship objectively will help you to grow as a person and potential partner. In effect, learning from your past relationship will help to ensure you don't make the same mistakes again. Explore these issues with your therapist. The further away you get from the divorce, and the more objective you can be about what went wrong, the more likely that you will be able to forgive your spouse – and yourself. Remember, forgiveness is not for anyone but you. It destroys the shackles that keep you tied to your past and releases you to move forward with your future.

If you are dating again, or thinking of dating again, remember that you are changing rapidly as a result of your emotional exploration. It's unlikely that relationships during this phase of your recovery will last long; rather, these may be transitional relationships – important as you try out the evolving you. It would be easy, and perhaps tempting, to jump into another long-term commitment or even marriage. Resist this urge. Remember that divorce rates are higher with each subsequent remarriage, in large part because people marry before having the opportunity to fully heal.

Rebuild Your Self-Esteem

As you do the work required to heal from your divorce, you will undoubtedly evolve in your thinking. You will become more self-aware, wiser, and more independent. You will become more objective about what went wrong and more mindful of what you now want. In short, you will begin to develop a new, different voice. Embrace this voice! It is the new, evolving you – more confident, wiser, and stronger. Along the way, you are rebuilding your self-esteem, likely bruised and battered following the divorce.

It is essential that you now surround yourself with people and activities that nurture your self-esteem by highlighting all the wonderful things about you. Are you creative? Funny? Nurturing? Tenacious? Find ways to honor these and other qualities you have. Find people who appreciate these things about you. I recall well the knot I would get in my stomach when with certain people following my separation. I quickly learned that I didn't have to spend time with those who made me feel worse instead of better. I began to set boundaries with anyone or anything that interfered with my healing. This included especially the well-meaning people who wanted to pry, judge, or control my thoughts and actions.

I began instead to pursue the people and activities in which I found joy and meaning. I found great solace in creative endeavors and dove into mastering oil painting. Through this solitary activity, not only did I develop my skills, but I also met others who appreciated my same sensibilities. I made new friends who knew me as an individual, not as a divorcing woman.

Slowly, I found "voice" in my paintings, expressing the woman I was becoming, strong and independent.

Embrace Your Power

As you embark on your journey, stop for a moment and take stock. No matter where you are in the divorce process, you're well on your way to a new future. You're becoming wiser, stronger and more independent as a result. You're also becoming more powerful.

In fact, as a single woman over 50, you're part of a paradigm shift – one that is placing unprecedented amounts of independence, power, and wealth in the hands of women. Expected to control two-thirds of the nation's wealth by the year 2030, women now have the historic opportunity to impact the world in ways that have never before been possible. Through philanthropy, public policy, and commerce we are gaining a collective voice, and a silver lining, from the circumstances giving rise to this phenomenon.

APPENDIX A

Historical Asset Class Performance

The chart on the following page provides a nice overview of how different types of assets (i.e. asset classes) have performed each year since 2002. Note that each colored tile represents a different type of asset. As expected, in some years, some assets do well, and in other years, they plummet, rotating from the top of the chart to the bottom.

The white tiles, on the other hand, represent a diversified portfolio of multiple asset types. While the diversified portfolio is never at the top of the chart, note that it's never at the bottom of the chart either. In fact, it provides a less volatile "ride" in the stock market while still returning a very respectable return of 6.9% per year over this 15-year period (2002-2016).

Asset Class Returns Chart Source: Barclays, Bloomberg, FactSet, MSCI, NAREIT, Russell, Standard & Poor's, J.P. Morgan Asset Management.
Large Cap: S&P 500, Small Cap: Russell 2000, EM Equity: MSCI EMF, DM Equity: MSCI EAFE, Comdty: Bloomberg Commodity Index, High Yield: Barclays Global HY Index,
Fixed Income: Barclays Aggregate, REITS: NAREIT Equity REIT Index.
The "Asset Allocation" portfolio assumes the following weights: 25% in the S&P 500, 10% in the Russell 2000, 15% in the MCSI EAFE, 5% in the MSCI EME, 25% in the Barclays Aggregate, 5% in the Barclays 1-3m Treasury, 5% in the Barclays Global High Yield Index, 5% in the Bloomberg Commodity Index and 5% in the NAREIT Equity REIT Index. Balanced portfolio assumes annual rebalancing. Annualized (Ann.) return and volatility (Vol.) represents period of 12/31/01-12/31/16. All data represents total returns for stated period. Past performance is not indicative of future returns. J.P. Morgan Asset Management *Guide to the Markets – U.S.* Data are as of December 31, 2016.

ASSET CLASS RETURNS

Rank	2002	2003	2004	2005	2006	2007	2008	2009	2010	2011	2012	2013	2014	2015	2016	2002-2016 Ann.	2002-2016 Vol.
1	Comdty. 25.9%	EM Equity 56.3%	REITs 31.6%	EM Equity 34.5%	REITs 35.1%	EM Equity 39.8%	Fixed Income 5.2%	EM Equity 79.0%	REITs 27.9%	REITs 8.3%	REITs 19.7%	Small Cap 38.8%	REITs 28.0%	REITs 2.8%	Small Cap 21.3%	REITs 10.8%	EM Equity 23.8%
2	Fixed Income 10.3%	Small Cap 47.3%	EM Equity 26.0%	Comdty. 21.4%	EM Equity 32.6%	Comdty. 16.2%	Cash 1.8%	High Yield 59.4%	Small Cap 26.9%	Fixed Income 7.8%	High Yield 19.6%	Large Cap 32.4%	Large Cap 13.7%	Large Cap 1.4%	High Yield 14.3%	EM Equity 9.8%	REITs 22.6%
3	High Yield 4.1%	DM Equity 39.2%	DM Equity 20.7%	DM Equity 14.0%	DM Equity 26.9%	DM Equity 11.6%	Asset Alloc. -25.4%	DM Equity 32.5%	EM Equity 19.2%	High Yield 3.1%	EM Equity 18.6%	DM Equity 23.3%	Fixed Income 6.0%	Fixed Income 0.5%	Large Cap 12.0%	High Yield 9.2%	Small Cap 20.7%
4	REITs 3.8%	REITs 37.1%	Small Cap 18.3%	REITs 12.2%	Small Cap 18.4%	Asset Alloc. 7.1%	High Yield -26.9%	REITs 28.0%	Comdty. 16.8%	Large Cap 2.1%	DM Equity 17.9%	Asset Alloc. 17.9%	Asset Alloc. 5.2%	DM Equity 0.4%	Comdty. 11.8%	Small Cap 8.5%	DM Equity 19.2%
5	Cash 1.7%	High Yield 32.4%	High Yield 13.2%	Asset Alloc. 8.1%	Large Cap 15.8%	Fixed Income 7.0%	Small Cap -33.8%	Small Cap 27.2%	Large Cap 15.1%	Cash 0.1%	Small Cap 16.3%	High Yield 7.3%	Small Cap 4.9%	Cash 0.0%	EM Equity 11.6%	Asset Alloc. 6.9%	Comdty. 19.0%
6	Asset Alloc. -5.9%	Large Cap 28.7%	Asset Alloc. 12.8%	Large Cap 4.9%	Asset Alloc. 15.3%	Large Cap 5.5%	Comdty. -35.6%	Large Cap 26.5%	High Yield 14.8%	Asset Alloc. -0.7%	Large Cap 16.0%	REITs 2.9%	Cash 0.0%	Asset Alloc. -2.0%	REITs 8.6%	Large Cap 6.7%	Large Cap 15.9%
7	EM Equity -6.0%	Asset Alloc. 26.3%	Large Cap 10.9%	Small Cap 4.6%	High Yield 13.7%	Cash 4.8%	Large Cap -37.0%	Asset Alloc. 25.0%	Asset Alloc. 13.3%	Small Cap -4.2%	Asset Alloc. 12.2%	Cash 0.0%	High Yield 0.0%	High Yield -2.7%	Asset Alloc. 8.3%	DM Equity 5.8%	High Yield 11.7%
8	DM Equity -15.7%	Comdty. 23.9%	Comdty. 9.1%	High Yield 3.6%	Cash 4.8%	High Yield 3.2%	REITs -37.7%	Comdty. 18.9%	DM Equity 8.2%	DM Equity -11.7%	Fixed Income 4.2%	Fixed Income -2.0%	EM Equity -1.8%	Small Cap -4.4%	Fixed Income 2.6%	Fixed Income 4.6%	Asset Alloc. 11.0%
9	Small Cap -20.5%	Fixed Income 4.1%	Fixed Income 4.3%	Cash 3.0%	Fixed Income 4.3%	Small Cap -1.6%	DM Equity -43.1%	Fixed Income 5.9%	Fixed Income 6.5%	Comdty. -13.3%	Cash 0.1%	EM Equity -2.3%	DM Equity -4.5%	EM Equity -14.6%	DM Equity 1.5%	Cash 1.3%	Fixed Income 3.5%
10	Large Cap -22.1%	Cash 1.0%	Cash 1.2%	Fixed Income 2.4%	Comdty. 2.1%	REITs -15.7%	EM Equity -53.2%	Cash 0.1%	Cash 0.1%	EM Equity -18.2%	Comdty. -1.1%	Comdty. -9.5%	Comdty. -17.0%	Comdty. -24.7%	Cash 0.3%	Comdty. 1.2%	Cash 0.8%

Your specific asset allocation will depend on how much you need to earn in order to meet your financial goals. Keep in mind, however, that an average 7% return over longer periods should normally more than protect your portfolio from inflation while allowing you the ability to sleep well at night.

Understanding Alternative Investments

As you accumulate more wealth, another way to diversify your portfolio is to allocate a percentage of your assets to alternative investments, defined as any investment that is not a traditional stock, bond, or short-term instrument such as a money market or certificate of deposit (CD). Below are some common types to consider:

Real Estate: Rental homes, shares in a larger property (apartments, office buildings, strip retail centers, etc.), shares in a mutual fund or exchange-traded fund that invests in stocks related to real estate – including REITs, shares in a real estate investment trust (REIT).

Mezzanine Lending: usually in diversified funds.

Smaller, mid-sized, and typically private companies often need external funding to expand their operations and continue to grow. While many of these companies may have attractive growth prospects and positive cash flows, they also often have more limited assets for collateral, and are thus unable to fully fund these expenditures from traditional lending sources, such as banks. Management may also be reluctant to sell more stock in the company, as this could materially dilute returns.

These situations create opportunities for investors (i.e. typically institutional or accredited investors) to provide funding to the company, often in the form of mezzanine debt at attractive rates. Mezzanine debt is generally unsecured debt and junior to bank debt or other senior debt (e.g. bond investors) while being senior to the company's equity or stock investors. This means that if something goes wrong with the business and the company is unable to fulfill all of its financial obligations, the banks and senior bondholders get paid back ahead of mezzanine debt investors, assuming there are sufficient assets.

In addition, mezzanine financing for some companies may involve higher leverage (i.e. amount of debt) which tends to increase overall risk. To compensate investors for this additional risk, companies tend to pay higher interest rates on the mezzanine debt as well as offer mezzanine debt investors the option to potentially acquire stock in the company based on certain conditions. Mezzanine debt is thus often seen as a bridge between equity and debt financing and also tends to be used frequently in corporate mergers and acquisitions.

Private Equity: usually in diversified funds.

Most investors are familiar with stocks of public companies that are traded on one of the major stock exchanges (e.g. The New York Stock Exchange). Such companies are required to report periodically on their financial conditions and business outlook so that the investing public can make informed decisions regarding the company's stock. Private companies (i.e. companies not listed on a major stock exchange), on the other hand, tend to be smaller, less-regulated businesses and are not required to make their financial data available to the public. Private equity investing is generally only available to institutional and accredited investors (investors with investable assets in excess of one million dollars or who meet certain income hurdles) via private placement offerings.

From an investor's perspective, private equity investing offers the potential to access managers who specialize in the private equity markets and potentially have more insight into investment opportunities than the general public. Private equity often involves investing in an existing business, with existing products and cash flows, and then restructuring the business so as to maximize its financial performance. The longer-term goal may be to sell the company later at a higher price or to eventually take the company public, via an Initial Public Offering (IPO) – an outcome that could be very rewarding to existing shareholders. Private equity investing can also involve taking a publicly-traded company private – a transaction referred to as a leveraged buyout.

While the potential returns from private equity investing can be very attractive, investors face additional risks due to the smaller, more opaque nature of private businesses. Not only do these investments often involve higher levels of debt or leverage, there is also increased risk that management may not be able to execute its plan to enhance the value of the business. For these reasons, private equity investing is a more aggressive investing strategy suitable for growth-minded investors who understand its various risks.

Venture Capital: a form of private equity investing, that tends to be more focused on early-stage, startup companies which may not yet be operational or have existing products (sometimes, the "company" may be no more than an idea). As an investor, venture capital is more about speculation and ultimately is a numbers game – most companies will likely fail, but the few that do succeed have the potential to be wildly successful. While investing in a diversified venture capital fund, as opposed to a single company, reduces risk somewhat, venture capital investing is one of the highest risk forms of investing. Remember, very few companies actually become a Facebook!

Alternative investments have become a favorite diversification tool for endowments and foundations in the last 20 years as a result of the entity's size and lifespan, which is realistically "forever." Many of the alternative investments above have limited or no liquidity for five to 10 years. The upside is that well-diversified alternative investments can provide returns similar to or even higher than stocks, but with less volatility from day to day or month to month. (Note: For some alternative investments, such as private real estate, this lower volatility is due in part to infrequent valuations. Because these investments are valued less frequently, their stated values may not reflect actual market pricing. With that said, some alternative investments, such as certain types of real estate, may also be inherently less volatile.) Again, because alternative investments are typically less correlated with traditional markets, they do offer another form of diversification and can play an important role in portfolios, depending on desired returns and levels of risk.

Many alternative investments also provide additional tax benefits: in the category of "it's not what you make, but what you keep." Having better after-tax returns becomes even more important as your portfolio grows from $2 million to $10 million and above.

What is the maximum to consider in alternative investments? Some endowments and foundations have as much as 40% to 60% of their investment portfolio in alternatives. This is fine if you have an infinite lifespan. As individual investors, however, an alternative investment allocation of 10% to 30% may be more appropriate, depending on circumstances and comfort level with the unique risks found in each alternative investment. Our normal safety protocol (again one of those rules of thumb that needs to be customized to your situation) is to limit the amount of illiquid securities based on economic conditions and your specific cash needs, with no more than 7% in any one fund and no more than 3% in a single property or investment. Obviously, these criteria can change from time to time and should be reviewed regularly.

Below are some sample allocations that include alternatives:

Conservative alternative to the traditional 60% stock/40% bond portfolio: 10% in cash; 20% in bonds; 60% in stocks; 10% in alternatives.

Moderate-risk option: 10% in cash; 25% in bonds; 45% in stocks; 20% in alternatives.

Aggressive-risk option: 5% in cash; 5% in bonds; 60% in stocks; 30% in alternatives.

Annuities are sometimes considered "alternative" investments, although many insurance agents consider them as "core" parts of a retirement income stream. Annuities can offer a lifetime stream of income, but can be quite expensive and yield low returns. If contemplating an annuity, have it analyzed by an objective advisor or CPA. Keep in mind that you're trading a future income stream for a current asset. For example, if you put $100,000 into an annuity, you might have a guaranteed income of $800 per month for the rest of your life. However, you will never get the $100,000 principal back.

Judy's perspective: *As my net worth grew, I began to explore investments beyond traditional cash, bonds, and stocks. As I became more knowledgeable, it was clear some investments were right for me and others didn't give me the same comfort level.*

Having rental homes was intriguing, but after talking to a number of people who owned rentals, the hidden costs of maintenance over time and having occasional vacancies didn't feel like a fit for me.

Given the below-average prospects for bonds in the coming decade as interest rates begin to rise, I decided on a target allocation of 60% stocks, 20% bonds, and 20% in alternative assets. My advisor and I have adjusted this approach over the years, although I don't seem to be spending less, as my parents did when they were my age.

It's clear that what has worked in the past needed to be adjusted for the changes in my generation. I'm sure my children and grandchildren will be adjusting in a similar way, depending on how the world evolves.

Disclaimer

Information presented in this book should not be considered a recommendation to buy or sell a particular security. Stearns Financial Group is an independent, registered investment advisor. More information about the advisor including its investment strategies and objectives is available at www.stearnsfinancial.com or upon request. The material presented here is not financial advice. It should not be assumed that any of the strategies discussed were or will prove to be profitable, or that the investment recommendations or decisions we make in the future will be profitable. Information was obtained from third party sources which we believe to be reliable but are not guaranteed as to their accuracy or completeness. The information in this book is for informational purposes only. In making an investment decision individuals should utilize other information sources and the advice of their investment advisor.